Fortune's Fool

Fortune's Fool

by Ivan Turgenev

adapted by Mike Poulton

THE OVERLOOK PRESS
WOODSTOCK & NEW YORK

First published in the United States in 2003 by
The Overlook Press, Peter Mayer Publishers, Inc.
Woodstock & New York

WOODSTOCK:
One Overlook Drive
Woodstock, NY 12498
www.overlookpress.com
[for individual orders, bulk and special sales, contact our Woodstock office]

NEW YORK:
141 Wooster Street
New York, NY 10012

Library of Congress Cataloging-in-Publication Data

Turgenev, Ivan Sergeevich, 1818-1883.
[Nakhlebnik. English]
Fortune's fool / Ivan Turgenev ; adapted by Mike Poulton.
p. cm.
I. Poulton, Mike. II. Title
PG3421.N3313 2003   891.72'3—dc21   2003054899

Book design and type formatting by Bernard Schleifer
Manufactured in Canada
ISBN 1-58567-451-6
1 3 5 7 9 8 6 4 2

for Alan

Introduction

For years friends, English and Russian, had been saying to me, "There's a wonderful play by Turgenev called *Impecuniousness.*" My stock response was always, "Does it live up to the promise of its title?" When I eventually tracked it down, I discovered it was a short and very funny farce about a spendthrift young aristocrat and his long-suffering valet. But this was not in fact the play my friends had been praising. As I was to discover, the "wonderful play" is, in the original, called *Alien Bread*—another Turgenev catchpenny title—and it was to become the basis for my reworking which I've called *Fortune's Fool.*

Some years ago the director David Hunt found in a bookshop in Malvern an English translation of a Turgenev play under the title *A Poor Gentleman*, which he thought I might enjoy. How right he was. The excellent translation, done in the early thirties, was by Constance Garnet, and is faithful to the language and—more important—the atmospherics of the original. Turgenev has always been favorite reading for me. I once started work on a radio adaptation of *Sketches from a Hunter's Album*, but became so absorbed in it I couldn't finish it. If I read a Turgenev short story, I end up reading another, and another, and then go on to the novels. The problem becomes one of stopping reading and starting writing.

It was Derek Jacobi who suggested I adapt *Alien Bread* for the Chichester Festival Theatre. My next move was to ask friends at Oxford to track down the original. They all started reading it too. "It starts off like Gogol and ends up like Ostrovsky," said one. "It's like early Chekhov in places," said another. I was, by this stage, becoming very excited. As they talked me through the Russian version, pointing out subtleties, double meanings, and giving me lectures on the historical background to the period, I began to realize just how good a piece it was, and how much more difficult it would be to adapt than I had originally imagined.

Turgenev is notoriously difficult for English-speaking audiences. A professor of Russian at Oxford went to a performance of Turgenev's *A Month in the Country* in London's West End. On his return he bumped

into the librarian of the Taylor Institute, Oxford's library of Eastern Eu-
ropean languages. "How did you enjoy *A Month in the Country?*" asked
the librarian. "A fortnight would have been long enough," replied the professor. It is a problem with novelists turned playwrights. Uncut, Chekhov's
Platonov would last about six hours, and Turgenev's *Month in the Country* almost as long as its title suggests. It was a problem with *Alien Bread.*
In the original the buildup to the arrival of the Yeletskys, with dozens of
servants—each with a good story to tell—lasts hours. How you cut a Turgenev play is as difficult and important as how you adapt it.

Most difficult of all is the problem of style. How do you pitch it? We
know so little about the style in which the original was played. In a sense
it's all Greek to a modern audience. Which provides a useful illustration.
A director looking at a work of Euripides, say, has what remains of the
text. It's like the libretto of an opera: we have the words but nothing of
the music, style of delivery, or choreography essential to the effect of the
original production. In some ways the problems with a Turgenev play are
more intractable. We have a raw text that promises much but doesn't give
up its secrets easily. We are dealing with a body of work that, in the main,
has never been seen in the English-speaking world. Directors familiar
with Chekhov may be tempted to treat the text like Chekhov and imagine that the same approach will do. But it won't. Or to put it another way,
an actor playing Hamlet can cheat a bit. He's probably seen the play, at
the very least, five or six times. There are five or six versions on film and
video. He can, if he's feeling desperate, add a bit of Jacobi, a bit of Olivier,
a bit of Ralph Fiennes to the rich stew of his creative juices. Their per-
formances, whether he likes it or not, inform his approach to the role. Not
so with Turgenev. With the exception of *A Month in the Country*, the
record is blank all the way back to the 1850's. There is, of course, no
sound recording, and the few photographs that exist of Russian perfor-
mances suggest a style something akin to that of early silent movies. So
that's no help. The challenge facing adapter, director, and actors is to try
to discover a modern interpretation of a style that produced the original
success. The excitement of it all is sharing in the process of discovery.

There are a few clues. We know Chekhov hated the stock characters
who littered the Russian stage—comic generals, blustering government
officials, idiotic serfs—because the moment they made an entrance the
audience knew exactly the sort of stage business and baggage they would
bring with them. But without the baggage and business, one is left with
very few starting points. While it's clear from his writing that Turgenev
must have shared Chekhov's dislike of stock characters and situations, it

remains more difficult to see from his texts alone how he improved matters. Or how his actors improved matters, as Turgenev spent most of his time out of Russia and missed most of his own first nights. Another clue is in the affection Chekhov felt for Turgenev's characters. We know the younger novelist and playwright admired Turgenev's ability to draw dramatic tension out of seemingly ordinary situations, and his genius for recreating the delights and horrors of everyday Russian life in a few phrases or sentences. Many of Chekhov's characters are prefigured in the plays and stories of Turgenev. But if we choose to approach Turgenev through Chekhov it's best to concentrate on the differences rather than the similarities. That should be our starting point.

When Turgenev wrote *Alien Bread* (1841), Russia was a vast, inefficient farm. About 96 percent of the population lived in the countryside, and 83 percent were agricultural laborers. The gentry were made up of just over 1 percent who owned outright over 50 percent of their fellow Russians.

Serfs produced the grain that was Russia's main export and the food everybody ate, and paid most of the taxes, but they had practically no rights and no personal freedom. A serf's life was dominated by three forces: the needs of the family, the demands of the mir—the village in which the peasantry were placed—and the overriding authority of the gentleman owner. The land was divided, usually inefficiently, into strips. The owner would allow his serf enough land to feed himself and his family. In return the serf had to work for his owner, or sell his crop in order to pay his owner rent. At any time the owner could revoke any rights he had allowed his serfs. He could take any of them into domestic service, treat them exactly as he liked, and decide whom they should marry. In many cases an owner would control the breeding of his serfs in much the same way as he bred his livestock. At the time in which the play is set, the system was in an advanced state of collapse, though the Emancipation Act that gave the serfs a measure of freedom did not come until twenty years later, in 1861.

By 1843 a government survey showed that over half the estates of Russia were mortgaged to various state departments. Private debt had reached alarming proportions, and, because of the complexity of inheritance laws, over the next twenty years over half the nobility would lose their lands and the serfs who worked them. The poor grew ever poorer, and the rich grew richer. Most of the surviving households of the period had impoverished relatives, friends, and hangers-on. Members of the same class tend to stick together. A gentleman left to starve would reflect badly on his peers. The instantly recognizable situation of the play's protagonist, Kuzovkin, is the rule rather than the exception, as is Waffles' in *Uncle Vanya*.

The estate Olga and Pavel have inherited in the play is like a small town or village. The effect of their arrival on the inhabitants is something like a change of government. A new regime is coming into power. There will be great changes. Pavel is a St Petersburg courtier, determined that his vast new estate will not go the way of Kuzovkin's and Vanya Ivanov's. So the return of Olga and Pavel must be very much more than just honeymoon or homecoming. It's time to take stock and study accounts.

The Russian word for hospitality—hospitality being a major theme of the play—is Khlebosol'stv, literally translated as "to honor with bread and salt." In Russia the custom was—and is—to welcome a visitor with the gifts of bread and salt—usually a large rye loaf with an indentation into which was fixed a little wooden dish of salt. The guest breaks off a piece of the bread, dips it in the salt, and says *Khleb da sol!* A householder— the dispenser of hospitality—is the giver of bread. Pavel, in his new role of estate owner, offers hospitality to both Kuzovkin and—with disastrous consequences—to Tropatchov. The "alien bread" of the title is the bread that Kuzovkin is forced to eat, having none of his own to offer anybody.

The meal that is eaten in the play is what we would call today a buffet. Roads were long and badly kept in Russia, and guests were often very late. *Zakusi*—Russian hors d'oeuvres—would be there to be eaten at any time. It may seem impolite to us that the lunch party starts without the hostess. It would have not seemed so in the period in which the play is set; in fact, it would have been impolite of Pavel and Olga to keep their guests waiting. Russians say that if you want to be well fed, you should sit next to the hostess. If you want to get drunk you should sit next to the host. The rules of hospitality required a host to see that the glasses of his guests were always refilled, and that each time wine was poured a new toast should be proposed. So the way in which Pavel's luncheon party starts out is nothing unusual. The same can be said for the way it ends.

I chose the title *Fortune's Fool*—from *Romeo and Juliet*—because I thought *Alien Bread* wouldn't say much to a modern audience. Kuzovkin is both the plaything of fortune and baffled by the complexities surrounding his own inheritance. When I finished my first draft, I showed it to Derek Jacobi. "What do you think of this, then? Is it Gogol, Ostrovsky, or Chekhov?" When he'd read it, he phoned me back. "It's Alan Bates," he said. Alan has become a hard act to follow. He created the role of Kuzovkin in *Fortune's Fool* and won three Best Actor awards, including the Tony. Frank Langella, as Tropatchov, won the Tony for Best Featured Actor and three other awards. All of which suggests that we'd got our little exercise in rediscovery about right.

MIKE POULTON
March, 2003

Fortune's Fool

Fortune's Fool was first produced at the Chichester Festival Theatre on August 27, 1996, with the following cast:

Kuzovkin	*Alan Bates*
Olga Petrovna	*Rachel Pickup*
Pavel Yeletsky	*Benedick Bates*
Tropatchov	*Desmond Barrit*
Karpatchov	*Richard Braine*
Ivanov	*David Collings*
Trembinsky	*John Turner*
Yegor	*John Bardon*
Pyotr	*Ashley Artus*
Vaska	*Alan Maher*
Ivanova	*Jean Challis*
Anpadist	*Jimmy Gardner*
Masha	*Mary Rose*
Director	*Gale Edwards*
Assistant Director	*David Hunt*
Décor	*Peter J. Davidson*
Lighting	*Mark L. McCullough*
Music	*Jason Carr*

A revised version of *Fortune's Fool* premiered at the Music Box Theatre in New York City on April 2, 2002. It was produced by Julian Schlossberg, Roy Furman, Ben Sprecher, Ted Tulchin, Aaron Levy, Peter Many, Bob Boyett, and James Fantaci, with the following cast:

Above Stairs (in order of appearance)

Vassily Semyonitch Kuzovkin	*Alan Bates*
Ivan Kuzmitch Ivanov	*George Morfogen*
Olga Petrovna	*Enid Graham*
Pavel Nikolaitch Yeletsky ("Paul")	*Benedick Bates*
Flegont Alexandrovitch Tropatchov	*Frank Langella*
Karpatchov ("Little Fish")	*Timothy Doyle*

Below Stairs (in order of appearance)

Praskovya Ivanova	*Lola Pashalinski*
Nartzis Konstantinitch Trembinsky	*Edwin C. Owens*
Pyotor	*Jeremy Hollingworth*
Servants	*Beth Bartley, Ann Ducati, Patrick Hallahan, John Newton*

Director	*Arthur Penn*
Set Designer	*John Arnone*
Costumes	*Jane Greenwood*
Lighting	*Brian Nason*
Sound	*Brian Ronan*
Music	*Kramer*

C a s t

above stairs:

VASSILY SEMYONITCH KUZOVKIN (mid-50's)—A gentleman who has fallen on hard times; a guest living on Olga Petrovna's country estate.

OLGA PETROVNA (21)—Heiress to a rich estate; she has just married:

PAVEL NIKOLAITCH YELETSKY (27)—A young aristocrat and member of the government; Olga's husband.

FLEGONT ALEXANDROVITCH TROPATCHOV (37)—A rich, boorish landowner and neighbor of the Yeletskys.

KARPATCHOV ("LITTLE FISH") (25)—Another impoverished young gentleman, who lives off Tropatchov.

IVAN ("VANYA") KUZMITCH IVANOV (45)—Another impoverished gentleman; Kuzovkin's best friend.

below stairs:

NARTZIS KONSTANTINITCH TREMBINSKY ("MUDDLER") (55)—The Yeletskys' incompetent steward, butler, and major domo; brutish and military.

PYOTR (20)—The footman; good at his job, a joker.

PRASKOVYA IVANOVA (65)—The old nanny and housekeeper; a hypocrite.

MAIDS, SERVANTS, SERFS, etc.

Act One

(*A rich country house in mid-19th-century Russia. The main playing area is a garden room with doors leading out to the extensive gardens. In the garden room, maids and footmen are hurriedly laying a table for a cele-bration lunch. Atmosphere of last-minute rush and some confusion. There is an inner stage, upstage—an inner hall, and beyond this a door leading to an entrance hall. In a window seat in the garden room is a folding table with a chess board on it.* TREMBINSKY, *the household's steward/butler, a bit of a bully, probably an ex-sergeant-major—his name means "balls-up" or more politely, "Muddler"—can be heard offstage yelling for* PYOTR *and shouting orders.* PRASKOVYA IVANOVA, *ex-nanny and now the housekeeper, comes to supervise the servants, who are putting the finishing touches to the laying of the table.*)

(*Enter* PRASKOVYA *with a maid.*)

PRASKOVYA

And why are there no flowers in the master bedroom? No—I don't want excuses— Just— You'd better see to it at once. And run! Must I do everything myself? (*to the servants*) Oh dear God! Isn't the table ready?

TREMBINSKY
(*enters followed by* PYOTR)
Get a move on, get a move on! Look at the time. Wake up lad!

PYOTR
Yes, sir. What shall I?—

TREMBINSKY
Oh no, no, no! I don't believe it! (*to* PRASKOVYA) Isn't that table set yet?

PRASKOVYA

(*ignoring* TREMBINSKY; *to a footman*)

Look at this fork. Is that a shine? Where's the shine? I want to see a shine. Polish it again—

TREMBINSKY

Look at the time! I said—

PRASKOVYA

I heard what you said. If you'd stop getting under everybody's feet we'd have been finished hours ago—

TREMBINSKY

I doubt that! If I—

PRASKOVYA

You're an old fool!—

TREMBINSKY

What did you call me!

PRASKOVYA

A fool! An old fool! A meddlesome old fool!

TREMBINSKY

Oh am I?—

PRASKOVYA

Yes—

TREMBINSKY

I'll tell you what I am—I'm in charge here, Praskovya Ivanova—

PRASKOVYA

In charge are you, Muddler? If things were left to you— Not on the table! (*to a maid*) Those aren't the table flowers—

TREMBINSKY

It's like talking to a brick wall! I might as well save my breath—I'm steward here, aren't I? If things aren't right it's me what gets blamed. Where's that lad—

PYOTR

Sir?

PRASKOVYA

(*to the maids*) Where are the napkins? Useless! The whole pack of you! Must I do everything myself! (*exit cursing, followed by maids*)

PYOTR

What do you want me to do?

TREMBINSKY

Just calm down! Look—any minute now the happy couple will walk through that door an' if everything's not as the new mistress wants it, it's me what'll get it in the neck . . . An' if I'm to get it in the neck I'm going to kick and flog you lot from here to Petersburg and back. Understood?

PYOTR *and* SERVANTS

Yessir!

PYOTR

Just tell me what—

TREMBINSKY

Shut up!

PYOTR

Shall I fetch the bread and salt?

TREMBINSKY

No! Not yet. Is the band ready?

PYOTR

Yes, but . . .

TREMBINSKY

What?

PYOTR

The only tune they know sounds like a funeral march.

TREMBINSKY

Holy St. Basil, pray for me! I don't want to know! Any minute they'll be coming up the path. (*to himself*) Have the paths been weeded? Is the grass cut?

PYOTR

Yes, sir. Paths, gardens— Everything's in order—saw to it my-

self. We went down to the village . . . loaded a cart with all the
kids, old folk, drunks— They've been hard at it for days.

TREMBINSKY

Hard at what?

PYOTR

Weeding. Gardening. Place looks a treat.

TREMBINSKY

Oh does it?

PYOTR

Yes, sir.

TREMBINSKY

Remind me again. Who you are?

PYOTR

What me?

TREMBINSKY

Yes you, you, you! Who are you?

PYOTR

You know me, sir. I'm Pyotr, sir.

TREMBINSKY

Oh no you're not! You're a footman, my boy, that's what you
are. You're indoors, below stairs, cleaning lamps and what
have you. You don't set foot outdoors if you know what's
good for you. Where the gardens start, you stop! It's not
your job to load carts with kids, the old folk, drunks and
what have you— Gardens is nothing to do with you. I wasn't
asking you. I was going to ask the head gardener. Fetch the
bread and salt.

PYOTR

Yes, sir. (*exit*)

TREMBINSKY

(*Watches* KUZOVKIN, *who comes through the hall
and makes his way toward his table in the window,
horrified at his presence, but unsure how to get rid of
him.* KUZOVKIN *is aware of* TREMBINSKY's *dilemma.
He bows politely—the gracious acknowledgment*

of an inferior by a superior. TREMBINSKY *nods
over-casually and turns his back.*)
Thinking of staying in here, was you?

KUZOVKIN

Hmm?

TREMBINSKY

Thing is . . . The young mistress and her new husband will be
arriving any minute.

KUZOVKIN

Yes . . . I know.

TREMBINSKY

Thinking of hanging around, was you? Going to present yourself?

KUZOVKIN

Of course.

TREMBINSKY

Think they'll be pleased to see you? . . . Is that your best suit?

KUZOVKIN

In fact it's my . . . (*He was going to say "only suit."*) Well . . .
I shall certainly be pleased to see her—them. (*Very faintly,
off, we hear the band rehearsing something that might be "The
Dead March" from* Saul.)

TREMBINSKY

I give up. Holy St. Basil pray for us all! Ah well . . . You'd better sit over there in the corner until they're ready for their
lunch. (KUZOVKIN, *amused, bows politely.*) Oh dear God! Listen to that— Pyotr! Pyotr! (*He runs towards the hall.*) Where's
the lad got to? (IVANOV, *a little nervous, has appeared in the
doorway. He is another impoverished nobleman.* TREMBINSKY
is not sure what to make of him.)

IVANOV
(*in the inner hall*)
I hope I'm not intruding.

TREMBINSKY
(*servile, not recognizing him*)
Not at all, sir, not at all. What was you wanting?

IVANOV

I'm Ivanov. Ivan Kuzmitch Ivanov—a friend of the gentleman over there—

KUZOVKIN

It's all right. He's with me.

TREMBINSKY

Wha—

KUZOVKIN

It's our neighbor. Ivanov. I invited him over—we have a game of chess to finish.

TREMBINSKY

Oh have you—did you! This is hardly the time and place for fun and games, gentlemen. (IVANOV *covered with confusion, tries to steal away.* PYOTR *comes charging in, past him.*) Where've you been? Can you play an instrument? Come with me. We've got to sort out this band. Lazy, good-for-nothings . . . (*This last is as much to* KUZOVKIN *and* IVANOV *as to* PYOTR. TREMBINSKY *and* PYOTR *exit.* IVANOV *lurks in the inner hall, more out than in.*)

KUZOVKIN

(*after a pause*)
Vanya? . . . Vanya!

IVANOV

What?

KUZOVKIN

You can come in here, Vanya. They've gone.

IVANOV

I think I'd better go too.

KUZOVKIN

Nonsense! What is there to be so nervous about?

IVANOV

That monster.

KUZOVKIN

Who? Muddler? Nartzis Konstantinitch I should say . . . He won't eat you.

IVANOV

I think he might try.

KUZOVKIN

Come over to the table. You'll feel safer here . . . in my corner.
Please. Sit down.

IVANOV

They're setting lunch. Shouldn't we get out of their way? Let's
go up to your room.

KUZOVKIN

Unfortunately my room is also the linen cupboard and just at
the moment it's full of housemaids pummelling eiderdowns.
We're fine here.

IVANOV

Could we not go over to my place, then?

KUZOVKIN

But why? No, Vanya, I must stay— I want you to stay too, so
sit down. Olga Petrovna is coming home at last—with her new
husband. Surely you want to meet them?

IVANOV

They won't want to meet me.

KUZOVKIN

How can you say that! Of course they will! All the way from
Petersburg . . . It's the first time she's been here for more than
six years. Nearer seven. Seven years! It's our duty to make her
feel welcome—her bridegroom too—aren't you curious to see
what he's like?

IVANOV

Not really. I imagine one bridegroom's much the same as any
other. Seen one, seen them all.

KUZOVKIN

Oh, Vanya!

IVANOV

Grinning like cats that've got the cream.

KUZOVKIN

Come on, sit down.

IVANOV

But what's the point, Vassily Semyonitch? They won't want to
be bothered with us—

KUZOVKIN

There. Sit. (*He does so, reluctantly.*) And don't let Nartzis
Konstantinitch intimidate you—all the noise and bluster—it's
what he's paid for. It's his job. I'm sure he's a good sort of fellow really. But don't forget—never forget: we are gentlemen.
They are only the servants.

IVANOV

I know. But do they see it like that?

KUZOVKIN

It's how we see things . . . That's what's important.

IVANOV

I suppose he's a rich man—the bridegroom?

KUZOVKIN

That I don't know. But he's the husband Olga Petrovna has
chosen, so he'll be a good man, a fine man. They say he's a
member of the government—highly thought of in Court circles.
It's what I would have wished for her.

IVANOV

What if he throws us out?

KUZOVKIN

What on earth do you mean, Vanya? Why should he throw us out?

IVANOV

Actually, I meant you, Vassily Semyonitch. What if he throws
you out? (*pause*) I'm sorry. Of course he wouldn't. Stupid of
me . . .

KUZOVKIN

No, Vanya, you're quite right. I must consider the possibility—

IVANOV

Oh, my friend—

KUZOVKIN

For the past few weeks, when have I not considered the possibility? Day and night . . . the worry of it all . . . Yes, it has to

be faced. Ha! Just look at the two of us—the state we're in:
both gentlemen—the best stock . . . both fallen on hard times
. . . but there is a difference. Whatever people may say of you,
you still have land—a home of your own—

IVANOV

That's what keeps me poor. Every penny of my income—and
more—much more—goes on that tottering, dilapidated, an-
cestral folly—maintenance and repairs—I'd be better to let it
fall down and move into the cowshed—

KUZOVKIN

But it's your home. It's yours . . . together with the good land
it stands on. I have nothing. For thirty years and more I've
lived on the charity of this family. Even the clothes I wear are
other people's cast-offs. Never anything of my own— Can you
imagine the effect that has had . . . on my . . . soul?

IVANOV

I know, I know. I'm sorry I said . . . Of course the new master won't throw you out. The old one didn't, did he? And what
a brute that man was! Nobody should have had to suffer as
you . . . There I go again! (*pause*) I'm sure they'll let you stay
on. (*pause*) He won't be like the rest of the Petersburg set.

KUZOVKIN

What do you mean?

IVANOV

You must know what they're like.

KUZOVKIN

What are they like?

IVANOV

Well you know—grasping, ruthless, heartless—lift any slimy
stone and you'll find the type—reptiles in fact—

KUZOVKIN

Vanya!

IVANOV

I don't wish to pre-judge him of course . . . He may be a perfectly decent sort of fellow—how would I know? I've never
met him—

KUZOVKIN

No, you haven't. (*a moment's silence*) Time will tell . . . time will tell. I can't believe that Olga Petrovna would marry any but the best of his kind. If you knew her as I do . . . she's everything that's gentle, and good, and noble. She'll speak up for me.

IVANOV

Oh I'm sure she will! Even though she's completely forgotten who you are? She was only a child when her mother died— How old was she?

KUZOVKIN

She was thirteen years and four months—

IVANOV

Yes, a child. And since then she's lived with her aunt in Petersburg. That sort of life changes people—hardens them. You remember only a little girl who shared her secrets with you, came running when she grazed her knees, brought you her dolls to repair—I'll bet you read her bedtime stories . . . but that sort of innocence fades, you know. So don't build up your hopes. I'm saying this because I don't want you to be hurt. Prepare yourself for the worst—She may not even recognize you . . . I'm sorry . . .

KUZOVKIN

You're wrong.

IVANOV

I hope so, but you'll see—

KUZOVKIN

That's enough, Vanya—

IVANOV

I was only—

KUZOVKIN

I don't want to discuss it.

IVANOV

Very well. (*pause*) It's just that—

KUZOVKIN

Stop it! Are we going to continue our game or not? Well? (IVANOV *remains silent*) Now don't be like that.

IVANOV

I'm not.

KUZOVKIN

Good. Especially as you were winning.
(*He begins to set up a chess end game, consulting a
notebook for the position of the pieces.*)

IVANOV

Was I?

KUZOVKIN

Mmm. I'd just lost a castle.

IVANOV

It doesn't seem right—

KUZOVKIN

What?

IVANOV

To be sitting here playing chess as if nothing's happened. Your
whole life's about to change—

KUZOVKIN

Don't start again, Vanya. Please! Pass me the box.

IVANOV

Hadn't you better go and find that man? The steward? Ask his
permission? He won't like it—

KUZOVKIN

We're not doing any harm, are we? We're in nobody's way.

IVANOV

Any minute now the happy couple will be arriving.

KUZOVKIN

And when they do we'll break off. Come on. It was your move.

IVANOV

They'll kick us out. (*pause*) The servants will be laughing up
their sleeves. The embarrassment will be excruciating. Are you
sure my knight was there?

KUZOVKIN

(*consults notebook*)
King's bishop four? Yes. It's right.

IVANOV

Oh. I thought it was too good to be true. (*He moves a piece.*)
Check.

KUZOVKIN

I was prepared for that. So . . . (*moves*)

IVANOV

Then you force me . . . to . . . (*moves*)

KUZOVKIN

Are you sure? I'll let you take it back if you want to.

IVANOV

Oh? What have I done now?

KUZOVKIN

The bishop. Look at the bishop.

IVANOV

Ah . . . Hmm . . . Well . . . (*Suddenly everybody in the hall,
offstage, is shouting. "They're here," "they're coming," etc.*
KUZOVKIN *and* IVANOV *don't react.*)

KUZOVKIN

(*pause*)
Do you think they're coming?

IVANOV

Probably just a rumor. Servants' hall gossip.

PYOTR

(*in the hall*)
I've got the bread and salt.

KUZOVKIN

(*suddenly nervous*)
Have I gone pale?

IVANOV

Pull yourself together. (*calling to* PYOTR) You lad! How do you
know they're coming?

PYOTR
(looking in from the hall)
The signal from the lodge's come. Old Mishka's on the roof waving his red flannel night-shirt. They're coming up the drive.

KUZOVKIN
Dear Lord!

TREMBINSKY
(enters, the hall perfectly calm for once; behind PYOTR*)*
What's going on?

PYOTR
They're coming up the drive.

TREMBINSKY
No they're not.

PYOTR
They are!

TREMBINSKY
No they're not, no they're not! It's a false alarm.

PRASKOVYA IVANOVA
(in the hall doorway)
Are they coming?

TREMBINSKY
No. It's a false alarm. *(hits* PYOTR*)* See what you've done. Tell 'em to relax—send 'em back to their posts. *(exit* PRASKOVYA IVANOVA*)*

PYOTR
But—

TREMBINSKY
Shut up!

PYOTR
But—

TREMBINSKY

Shut it! Get up to the attic and watch for the signal. When they pull into the drive Old Mishka will wave his red night-shirt from the roof of the lodge.

PYOTR

He is. He has.

TREMBINSKY

What!

PYOTR

That's what I'm saying. He's waving it.

TREMBINSKY

What! He can't be! Why wasn't I told! (*He runs off, followed.*) They're coming! They're coming! They're coming! (*shouts from off: "No they're not," "They're not," "It's a false alarm!" etc.*) They are! They are!

PYOTR
(*enters the garden room, carrying a tray with the traditional welcoming gift of a huge ring of bread and salt and puts it on the table*)

I think they might be coming.

PRASKOVYA IVANOVA
(*in the doorway*)

Are they coming?

PYOTR

Mishka's sent the signal.

PRASKOVYA IVANOVA
(*shouting off*)

To your places, girls. To your places. (*off*) Where's the bread and salt?

TREMBINSKY
(*pushing past her, followed*)

Pyotr! Pyotr! Where's the bread and salt?

PRASKOVYA IVANOVA

Where's the bread and salt?

TREMBINSKY
(PYOTR *turns and shows the tray.*)

Well why aren't you out on the front steps?

PYOTR

All right! All right! Calm down! (*He goes out into the hall.*
PRASKOVYA IVANOVA *is shepherding as many maids as is practi-
cable, all in their best dresses, into the hall. They collide with*
PYOTR, *who manages not to drop the tray.*) Steady on! Watch it!

PRASKOVYA IVANOVA

In here, girls. Line up in here.

TREMBINSKY

No, not in here! What are you playing at, woman? Get 'em
lined up on the front steps!

PRASKOVYA IVANOVA

Masha said you said in here!

TREMBINSKY

I never said anything of the sort! Out! Out! Out! Fetch the
band! Musicians to their places. Where's the foreman?

(*Great confusion in the hall. Noises off: shouts of "They're here!" "Where's
the foreman?" "Bread and salt." etc. "Quiet!" "Shhhh!"*)

TREMBINSKY

(*off*) Everybody! Shut up! (*silence*)

IVANOV

I'm going too—while there's still time to get away.

KUZOVKIN

No you're not.

(*Silence.* KUZOVKIN *is almost overcome with emotion.* IVANOV *is puzzled
by this. Suddenly the band starts playing, badly and out of tune. The
sound of a carriage drawing up. Conversation. The band fizzles out. More
laughter.*)

OLGA

(*off*) This way! In here! (*Then into the hall, laughing,* OLGA
PETRONOVA *with an armful of flowers followed by* YELETSKY,
her husband, who is holding the bread and salt. Then in come
TREMBINSKY, PRASKOVYA IVANOVA, *and* PYOTR. *The other servants wait in the doorway.*) At last! At last. Come in, Paul.
Come here. Welcome to your home. Dear, enchanted old
house. Magical home! After seven years . . . Don't worry, I'll be

sensible again in a moment—but just now! (*to the servants*)
Thank you, thank you, thank you! For making everything so
perfect—your welcome—the wonderful band! (*They all come
into the garden room.*)

TREMBINSKY

Well—

OLGA

Everything! Perfection! Just as I wanted it. (*to* YELETSKY,
laughing) Oh give it back to him, Paul—you look ridiculous!
(YELETSKY *gives the huge bread ring and the salt to* PYOTR,
who is not sure what to do with it. OLGA *hands the flowers to*
MASHA, *then runs and hugs* YELETSKY, *laughing.*) This is your
master. You must love him as I love him, and do everything in
your power to make him love his new home. Love! (*She
weeps.* YELETSKY *hugs her. They seem to forget for a moment
that there are other people on stage.*)

TREMBINSKY

Will you be needin' a bite . . . er . . . to eat? Glass of tea perhaps? Something after your long journey?

OLGA

No. No thank you. Not for the moment. (*to* YELETSKY) I'm
going to show you every inch of the house—I can't wait to see
you sitting in your study—you simply have to love it—every
book, every nook, every cranny—

YELETSKY

I do—

OLGA

What?

YELETSKY

I love it already.

OLGA

But how can you? You haven't seen it yet—

YELETSKY

I love it because you love it.

IVANOV

(*to* KUZOVKIN)
What did I tell you? Like a cat that's got the cream . . .

OLGA

Oh Paul! It's not enough. Love things for what they are. Not just for my sake.

PRASKOVYA IVANOVA
(*taking* OLGA's *hat and coat*)
Oh dear lady! Oh my darling child! (OLGA *smiles and hugs her.*)

OLGA

Nanny. You don't seem a day older—the house is older—the trees in the drive are much, much taller than when I left them—but you're exactly as I remember you—just the same. God bless you!

PRASKOVYA IVANOVA

Oh my darling!

OLGA

This room's much smaller though. Much smaller— It used to be enormous!

YELETSKY

No—you've grown up—that's all. The last time you stood here you were a little girl. I doubt you could reach the window sills—

OLGA

What nonsense! I was thirteen years old.

KUZOVKIN
(*to himself*)
And four months. (*She hears him and approaches him. He goes up to her.*) Olga Petrovna, may I . . . (*His voice breaks.*)

OLGA
(*slowly remembering*)
Vassily? . . . Vassily Petrovitch? How lovely to see you. How kind of you to be here. (*She is a little more reserved than her language suggests.*)

KUZOVKIN

Dear child—Dear lady—I . . .

OLGA

You must forgive me. I didn't see you at first—hiding away in the corner—

KUZOVKIN

Yes—will you allow me— (*kisses her hand*) I'm so happy to see you. Please ignore the odd tear or two that seem to have . . .

OLGA

Paul, come here. I want you to meet Vassily Petrovitch, our dear, dear friend.

YELETSKY

(*bows*)
Delighted.

KUZOVKIN

(*bows.* IVANOV *also bows, but nobody has noticed him yet.*)
Happy man! . . . Many congratulations . . . We are all—so . . . happy for you both . . . Er, may I . . . (*He goes over to* IVANOV.)

YELETSKY

(*to* OLGA)
Who is he?

OLGA

(*amused*)
Shhh! He lives here.

KUZOVKIN

. . . Present my good friend, your neighbor, Ivan Kuzmitch Ivanov?

YELETSKY

Delighted. (*bows*)

OLGA

And my friend too, I hope.

IVANOV

Dear lady. (*bows*)

OLGA

You're very welcome here. But just for a moment you must excuse us both. I promised myself that the first thing I would do was show my husband his home.

KUZOVKIN

Of course you must.

YELETSKY

Forgive me, gentlemen. (*they bow*)

OLGA

That's enough bowing! They're friends! Come on, Paul, you must see everything. This is where I was born—where I grew up. I won't wait!

YELETSKY

I'm coming. (*to* TREMBINSKY) Tell my valet to bring the boxes in, would you?

TREMBINSKY

Of course, sir, naturally, count on me . . .

OLGA

Oh come on! (*She exits, followed by* YELETSKY.)

TREMBINSKY

Right, you lot. Back to work. Any minute now they'll be wanting their lunch—you mark my words—once they stop billing and cooing, they'll need their feed—come on, jump to it. Follow me.

PYOTR

I'd stay in the hall if I was you, Nartzis Konstantinitch. He'll need to talk to you about the estate.

TREMBINSKY

Oh? (*horrified*) Do you think so?

PYOTR

First thing he'll want to know is how much they're worth. Stands to reason, dunnit? (*The men go out.*)

PRASKOVYA IVANOVA
(*shepherding out the girls*)
Back to work, girls. The show's over. What you laughing at, Masha? (*exit*)

TREMBINSKY
(*in the doorway*)
Are you staying in here?

KUZOVKIN

Yes?

TREMBINSKY

You're not going out then?

KUZOVKIN

No.

TREMBINSKY

Well don't blame me, that's all. (*exits into hall*) It's nothing to
do with me.

KUZOVKIN

Extraordinary fellow! (*then, suddenly*) Well? Tell me! Come
on! What do you think of her, Vanya? Eh? Isn't she amazing,
stunning, a ray of the purest sunlight? What do you say? And
hasn't she grown! Hmm? Oh she's so . . . So . . . And her . . .
Don't you think so? Ha! So she's forgotten me, has she? Yes!
That's what you said, wasn't it? But I never doubted her for a
minute, and I was right to trust her. Confess! You were wrong.
Why can't you admit it?

IVANOV

Well—

KUZOVKIN

Tell me I was right.

IVANOV

Give me a chance!

KUZOVKIN

Sorry.

IVANOV

So why did she call you Vassily Petrovitch?

KUZOVKIN

Oh come on! Come on! After six—nearly seven years! Is that
all you can say? Vassily Petrovitch, Vassily Semyonitch—it's all
the same—anybody could make that mistake—Simon, Peter—
it's the same name—surely you see that, Vanya? But look how
she treated me—how pleased she was to see me—and the way
she introduced me to her husband—"our dear, dear, friend"—
and what a fine man he is—what? A real gentleman. You can
see why he's so well liked at Court. Don't you agree, Vanya?

IVANOV

I don't know what to say, Vassily Semyonitch. Petersburg folk
. . . Petersburg manners . . . Who can tell what they're really
thinking? I just don't know. I'd better go home.

KUZOVKIN

Vanya! What's the matter? This is so unlike you. Why do you
want to run away? She said you were welcome here.

IVANOV

She said it, yes. But I'm not sure if I feel it.

KUZOVKIN

Nonsense! It's Nartzis Konstantinitch—it's him you're scared of.

IVANOV

Not any more. It's you I'm thinking about, Vassily. I'm afraid
for you.

KUZOVKIN

But why!

IVANOV

I've told you. I don't know. I just feel it.

KUZOVKIN

Well you can stop feeling it. Don't be so foolish. Calm down—
and tell me what I really want to hear—which is what you
think of her. Just talk—about her! I want to hear you talking
about her. Say whatever comes into your head.

IVANOV

She's all right, I suppose.

KUZOVKIN

All right? All right! Is that the best you can do? Tell me
about—her smile! Her smile alone is beyond price. And her
voice? What can I say—

IVANOV

Well, I—

KUZOVKIN

To me her voice is like birdsong in the deepest night, when
everything else is still and silent. You see, Vanya, she inspires
such love in people—because she is so loving herself. She

adores her husband, as he does her. My heart went out to
them— You must have felt that too, Vanya? Did you not feel it?

IVANOV

If you say so.

KUZOVKIN

Oh no, it's too much! Why do you have to bring me down so?
For once I'm utterly, completely happy, and you have to go
and spoil it. Why are you doing this?

IVANOV

I can't help it! Shhh. They're coming back. (*enter* OLGA *and*
YELETSKY)

OLGA

It's no palace, but, such as it is, it's yours—all yours.

YELETSKY

Ours. It's a fine old house. It has great dignity, but I feel it's
smiling upon us. I truly love it.

OLGA

And now you must see the garden.

YELETSKY

Yes, I must. But first I ought to have a word with your steward—I think he's expecting it. He's waiting in the hall.

OLGA

My steward? (*reproachfully*)

YELETSKY

Ours! (*kisses her hand*) I mean ours.

OLGA

Well don't let him keep you long. Vassily Petrovitch, you'll come
into the garden with me, won't you? Please say you will—

KUZOVKIN
(*This is almost too much for him.*)
But of course—I'd be delighted.

OLGA

And you, dear friend? I know you'll come with us.

IVANOV

Why not.

YELETSKY

Put your coat on, Olga.

OLGA

Don't fuss, Paul! I don't need a coat. I'm home. Give me your arm, Vassily Petrovitch.

KUZOVKIN
(*unable to believe his good fortune*)

My arm?

OLGA

Don't worry, I'll give it back. Like this. See. (*She takes his arm.*) Don't say you've forgotten . . . (*exit all but* YELETSKY, *who watches them go, smiles, then crosses to the door.* PYOTR *enters with flowers for the table.*)

YELETSKY

Er . . . Boy.

PYOTR

Yessir?

YELETSKY

I can't call you boy. Feels stupid. What's your name?

PYOTR

Pyotr, sir.

YELETSKY

Good. Well then, Pyotr. That fellow in the hall—?

PYOTR

Muddler, sir—I mean Nartzis Konstantinitch—

YELETSKY

Yes, the steward. Ask him to come in, would you? I think he's hoping for a word with me.

PYOTR

Oh he is, sir. Of course, sir.

YELETSKY

Thank you, er . . . (*trying to remember*) ?

PYOTR

Pyotr, sir.

YELETSKY

Pyotr. That's right. Thank you.

PYOTR

Pleasure, sir. (*He exits. A moment later* TREMBINSKY *enters.*)

YELETSKY
(*suddenly very businesslike*)
Ah, Nartzis Konstantinitch. Tomorrow . . . yes, tomorrow I shall
begin to go over Olga Petrovna's estate. Lands, books, accounts . . .

TREMBINSKY

Yes, sir.

YELETSKY

And I need a little preliminary information. Tell me—how
many serfs do we have?

TREMBINSKY

Three hundred and eighty-four, sir. Men that is.

YELETSKY

Good, good—

TREMBINSKY

At least there was at the last census.

YELETSKY

Oh? But that was nine years ago, wasn't it?

TREMBINSKY

About that, sir. Nine—Yes, I think it was about nine years ago. I—

YELETSKY

And the number is still three hundred and eighty-four?

TREMBINSKY

Well, maybe more by now . . .

YELETSKY

How many more?

TREMBINSKY

Oh, a good few, sir.

YELETSKY

Hmmm . . . Well I'd like you to find out the exact number and let me know as soon as you can.

TREMBINSKY

Of course, sir.

YELETSKY

These things must be done properly.

TREMBINSKY

Yessir.

YELETSKY

Now tell me about the land. Is it in a single block or is it split into several areas?

TREMBINSKY

Er . . . A single block, sir. Though there is one or two outlying villages here and there, as it were . . . Only a few, though. It's mainly all together . . .

YELETSKY

I think I see. And how much of the estate would you say is good farmland?

TREMBINSKY

Oh, lots of it.

YELETSKY

Can you be a little more precise?

TREMBINSKY

Eight hundred and fifty acres. (YELETSKY *is taken aback*.) Roughly.

YELETSKY

You're just guessing, aren't you?

TREMBINSKY

What, me, sir? No, sir.

YELETSKY

And land that isn't under the plough? How much of that is there?

TREMBINSKY

Well, there, sir, I confess you've got me. Difficult to say, isn't it? There's the scrub—and those bits down the side of the valleys—and then you'd have to count in the farmers' vegetable patches and what have you—and the meadows too—there's some good land down to hay . . .

YELETSKY

But I'm going to need accurate figures—

TREMBINSKY

Thing is, sir—it's never been properly measured, has it? There may be an old plan or two somewhere with that sort of information on it, what the old master kept—but if you was to ask for my best guess, I'd say that the land not down to crops amounts to about four hundred and fifty acres, maybe.

YELETSKY

I'm afraid your best guess won't do. First thing in the morning I want you to set everything else aside and prepare a detailed survey of the whole estate. Do you understand?

TREMBINSKY

Yes, sir.

YELETSKY

Is there any forest?

TREMBINSKY

Oh yes, sir. That I do know. I have the figures from the head forester. There are five hundred and eighty-four acres and a half of the finest timber.

YELETSKY

Good! It's a start. So, all in all there are about, what?—fifteen hundred—two thousand acres?

TREMBINSKY

Fifteen hundred! Bless you, sir—it's over six thousand—well over. Everybody knows that!

YELETSKY

But you told me . . . (*stops, knowing it's pointless*) Never mind. We'll sort this out tomorrow. I must have everything in proper order or . . . You know what I'm saying, don't you?

TREMBINSKY

Yes, sir.

YELETSKY

Well then. One thing more. Tell me about the peasants here.
Are they happy? Well looked after?

TREMBINSKY

Oh yes, they're a good lot, sir. They don't give no trouble.
They know better than that.

YELETSKY

Hmmm . . . But they are well provided for? Does somebody
see that they have all they need—doctors, teachers, moral
guidance, that sort of thing?

TREMBINSKY

Guidance? Oh yes, sir. Best of everything. They know when
they're well off.

YELETSKY

Hmm . . . Good. Anyway . . . I shall see for myself tomorrow.
I think that's all. No, before you go. tell me, please, about the
gentleman who lives here.

TREMBINSKY

What, Kuzovkin? Vassily Semyonitch Kuzovkin. He's just a
poor gentleman, sir. Down on his luck. He's lived here since
the old master's time. Old master gave him a roof. Kept him
for . . . how shall I put it? Sort of court jester. His fool. There
has to be someone to make fun of, doesn't there?

YELETSKY

I would have to disagree. How long did you say he's been here?

TREMBINSKY

Well, the old man—the old master's been dead over twenty
years, hasn't he? So I'd say, what?—twenty-five, thirty years . . .

YELETSKY

Good Lord! Well, well . . . (*pause*) I suppose there's an estates
office?

TREMBINSKY

Oh yes, sir.

YELETSKY

I'll meet you there tomorrow—at five.

TREMBINSKY

Five in the morning, sir? (YELETSKY *just stares at him*) Right, sir.

YELETSKY

I think you'd better go. You have a great deal to attend to. That's all. For now. I hope there's something good for lunch.

TREMBINSKY

Thank you, sir. (*exit*)

YELETSKY

Is it possible that anybody could be so stupid? Had he been born a gentleman, he'd have been a cabinet minister by now. Or a field marshall at least. I thought Petersburg had the monopoly on such fellows. But we shall see. (*crosses to look out into the garden*) I think I could grow to like life in the country—my own estate. Lord of all I survey. Away from Court and the nincompoops who gather there—

TROPATCHOV

(*off*) They're here! I don't believe it! At last!

YELETSKY

Oh no. More visitors . . .

PYOTR

(*at the door*)

Sir, your neighbor, Flegont Alexandrovitch Tropatchov, has called upon you. Will you see him?

YELETSKY

The name's familiar. Who did you say he was?

PYOTR

Flegont Alexandrovitch Tropatchov, sir?

YELETSKY

Our neighbor?

PYOTR

Yes, sir. He owns most of the land round here—apart from your own, sir.

YELETSKY

Thank you, Pyotr. You'd better ask him in.

PYOTR

At once, sir.

TROPATCHOV

(*entering with a flourish. He speaks rapidly and largely for his own entertainment.*)

My dear! How wonderful to see you! Bonjour, bonjour, dear Pavel Nikolaitch, buon giorno—ten thousand welcomes! (*pause*) No! I don't believe it! He doesn't remember me! Surely dear sir?—At Count Kuntsov's? The regimental ball? I was a humble addition to the glittering melee attendant upon His Imperial Majesty, the Tsar. Remember? You were presented. I smiled at you.

YELETSKY

Oh yes . . . Of course . . . Delighted to see you again . . .

TROPATCHOV

And now fate marks us out to be the best of friends! I'm your nearest neighbor, don't y'know? Practically every day my carriage sweeps past your gate—but no longer, no longer! I shall be forever on your doorstep! My dear, the whole district has been simply aching for your arrival—we've known for some time you were on the way—and, by complete chance I was running up to town and something—some impulse—an inspiration—made me decide to call in person in order to ascertain from your blockheads when, exactly, you were expected, and— imagine my surprise!— Here you are! Dear Pavel Nikolaitch!

YELETSKY

I—

TROPATCHOV

But you must tell me, instantly, if this is not a good moment— I won't be offended—I know how things are. You need time to settle in. So just say the word and I'm gone! Poof! Entre gens of our class, y'know, comme il faut and what have you.

YELETSKY

Not at all, not at all—it's a very good time. I hope you'll allow me to offer you some lunch—though I can't say what they might give us. I'm not sure how well one eats in the country.

TROPATCHOV

Well there, my dear, you need have no fears. We don't stint ourselves out here, I assure you, and in this house everything has always been carried off with impeccable style. Haute cuisine—tres, tres haute—cordon blue I promise you. That's the real reason I called on you! (laughs)

YELETSKY

Oh I—

TROPATCHOV

No! You must forgive ma petite jest. Truly, though, my own chef trained in Paris, so I hope you will do me the honor one day soon . . . very very soon . . .

YELETSKY

Is—

TROPATCHOV

My dear, I can't tell you how enchanting it is to have you among us—You et Madame—cher petite Madame— How *is* she, by the by—sweet, sweet thing? My worst fear, my nightmare, is that you'll find us all so very dull—so very, very dull—and you'll scurry away back to Petersburg, flippety floppety, like a pair of little grey rabbits? Hmmm?

YELETSKY

Oh, I—

TROPATCHOV

And who could blame you? I must confess that we have so little society in the country. One has to make do with what one can find. Good breeding, good manners, good fellows—all in such terribly short supply. As for wit, conversazione, et tous les autres petite diversions—well, my dear, you can forget them.

YELETSKY

Really—

TROPATCHOV

Am I boring you?

YELETSKY

Certainly not! Not at all.

TROPATCHOV

And how is your wife? Poverina! To lose first her father and then her mother— I used to be so very fond of the dear little thing—though now of course she will be a fine lady. I expect she's forgotten me.

YELETSKY

No! I'm sure you're wrong! Who could forget . . . She'll be overjoyed to see you again . . . Er . . . She's in the garden at the moment with . . . with a gentleman who—it would appear—lives with us—

TROPATCHOV

Oh him! Surely he's not still here? My dear, what a bore for you—

YELETSKY

He seems a decent enough sort of chap—

TROPATCHOV

How insensitive of him to intrude on your homecoming! Your late dear father-in-law's tame fool and whipping boy, wasn't he? I'm surprised he dare show his face—pushing in where he's not wanted when you've so many demands on your time. By the way—I've brought another gentleman along—more our sort, but not quite the thing if you understand me—I left him outside in the hall—

YELETSKY

But why! You must bring him in at once—

TROPATCHOV

Oh, he'll come to no harm—he's of no consequence. I keep him by me because he's lost his fortune—a bankrupt you know—barely presentable—but he amuses me. It's such a bore to go about on one's own, and acts of charity can be so delicious, don't you find?—so I—give him an airing now and then. But waste no time on him, dear sir, je vous en prie. (*goes to the door*) Karpatchov! Venez ici old chap. (KARPATCHOV *comes in and bows.*) Here he is, Pavel Nikolaitch, he's yours to command . . .

YELETSKY
I'm pleased to make your acquaintance, sir.

TROPATCHOV
(*takes* YELETSKY *by the arm and steers him away from*
KARPATCHOV, *who looks humbled and stands aside*)
C'est bien, c'est bien—that's enough of him. Tell me, my dear,
do you intend to stay with us long?

YELETSKY
I have three months' leave of absence—

TROPATCHOV
Oh, shame! That's no time at all! But I do so understand—the
demands of high office—the Tsar is a jealous mistress, as
t'were—I'm surprised he could spare you at all.

YELETSKY
Really, Flegont Alexandrovitch, I'm sure the Ministry will
manage perfectly well—

TROPATCHOV
Nonsense! Nonsense! But in the short time you are spared to
us we must make sure that dull moments are few. Do you
shoot?

YELETSKY
I've never fired a gun in my life—but I'd like to. And I did buy
a couple of hounds before I left Petersburg—

TROPATCHOV
Dogs. One hunts with hounds and shoots with dogs. Don't worry,
we'll undertake to make a sportsman of you, won't we, Little Fish?

KARPATCHOV
Yes, sir.

TROPATCHOV
It's what I call him. Leetle Feesh! Tomorrow or the day after we
could drive over to Malinnik? Walk up, don't you think?—spot
of rough shooting? What's the game like at Milinnik this year?

KARPATCHOV
Doing well, sir—very well. It's better at Kamenny Gryada
though—

TROPATCHOV

Oh?

KARPATCHOV

Fedul, the gamekeeper was saying that over in Goryelye . . .
(OLGA *comes in from the garden, laughing, with* KUZOVKIN
and IVANOV. KARPATCHOV *stops speaking and bows.*)

OLGA

Paul, you must come outside at once . . .

YELETSKY

Olga, my dear. Allow me to introduce—

TROPATCHOV

No need! No need! It's me, Tropatchov—we're old, old friends.
Dear Olga Petrovna, have I changed so much? Don't you recog-
nize me? Tropatchov—your neighbor! Flegont Alexandrovitch
Tropatchov! I was at your christening!

OLGA

Oh, Monsieur Tropatchov . . . of course I remember you.
(*gives him her hand*)

TROPATCHOV

Welcome home!

OLGA

Isn't it wonderful! I don't think I could be happy anywhere but
here.

TROPATCHOV

Don't let the gilded youth of Petersburg hear you say that!

OLGA

(*smiles*)
I've been reliving my childhood—all my most cherished mem-
ories— Paul, you must see the garden—there's a cherry stone
I planted that's grown into a huge tree—

YELETSKY

This is Monsieur Karpatchov, another neighbor. (KARPATCHOV
bows and retires.)

OLGA

How do you do, sir.

TROPATCHOV

Oh don't bother with him. I want you all to myself—both of you. The last time I saw dear Olga Petrovna she was comme ça *(indicating height)* and now—Behold! The mistress of a great estate. The whirligig of time, my dears—oh, what a whirligig it is!

OLGA

I hope you'll stay for lunch.

TROPATCHOV

Of course you do, and I'd be delighted.

YELETSKY

I have already asked Monsieur Tropatchov, my dear. I only hope that we have something decent to offer him—

TROPATCHOV

Oh please don't worry so—a crust would suffice—*(confidentially, to* YELETSKY) The intruders? You don't want them around, do you? Shall I get rid of them?

YELETSKY

Oh no . . . They seem pleasant enough—

TROPATCHOV

As you wish. *(goes over to* KUZOVKIN *and the others)* We've not been introduced. How are you?

KUZOVKIN

How do you do.

TROPATCHOV

Do you know this gentleman? *(indicating* KARPATCHOV)

KUZOVKIN

I—

TROPATCHOV

Karpatchov. My friend Karpatchov. Oh, are you here too?

IVANOV

Yes. I'm here too.

TROPATCHOV

Damned if I can remember your name—

OLGA

Monsieur Tropatchov—er, gentlemen—

TROPATCHOV

Madame?

OLGA

Please don't think me rude if I leave you for a moment—we
have only just arrived . . . and I must —

TROPATCHOV

My dear, of course you must. Run along, run along—and you
too, Pavel Nikolaitch, if you wish—no standing on ceremony,
we're old friends. Treat the place as your own! (*laughs*) I shall
amuse myself with these . . . gentlemen.

OLGA

I'll change out of these traveling clothes—

TROPATCHOV

I know, I know! The mirror calls. I'm the very last person to
come between a lady and her dressing table. I know exactly
how you must feel. (*laughs*)

OLGA

You have a wicked tongue, Monsieur!

TROPATCHOV

Famous for it!

OLGA

I must leave you gentlemen. Forgive me. (*exit*)

TROPATCHOV

My dear, I must congratulate you once again. She is enchanting! All peaches and champagne sorbet—exquisite! Magnifique!

YELETSKY

Yes—

TROPATCHOV

You are, dear sir, a very lucky man.

YELETSKY

Oh I know.

TROPATCHOV

(*giving* KUZOVKIN *and* IVANOV *a hard look*)

Look, if I'm really not keeping you, perhaps you would allow me to show you something of your estate.

YELETSKY

Well—

TROPATCHOV

Just for a moment, while they bring lunch? The sawmill's just beyond the garden wall, and there should be men at work on the threshing floor, too. What say we pay them a surprise visit?

YELETSKY

Well—

TROPATCHOV

I have a genius for estate management. I might be able to give you a pointer or two.

YELETSKY

Well, if you really wouldn't mind. Where's my hat . . .

TROPATCHOV

I'd be delighted—let's go! Pyotr! (*at the door*) Little Fish, you'll come with us, I think—

PYOTR

(*at the door*)

Yes, sir?

YELETSKY

Pyotr—

TROPATCHOV

Your master and I are going to take a turn round the threshing floor and the sawmill. We shan't be long. Tell Trembinsky to bring lunch. (*nods casually at* KUZOVKIN *and* IVANOV) Gentlemen. (*exit all but* KUZOVKIN *and* IVANOV)

KUZOVKIN

Well?

IVANOV

All right! All right! I like her a lot. Almost certainly she's quite wonderful.

KUZOVKIN

She's so . . . giving.

IVANOV

Unlike her husband.

KUZOVKIN

Oh! What's wrong with him?

IVANOV

I don't like the company he keeps.

KUZOVKIN

Well, what else could he do? You can't take against him for the way Tropatchov behaves—the poor man's only just arrived. He'll choose his friends more carefully when he gets to know people.

IVANOV

I think he's cold-hearted.

KUZOVKIN

Great heavens, Vanya! How could you possibly say that? He appears . . . formal—because he's accustomed to Petersburg society. It's probably the way things are done at Court. You can't expect him to throw his jacket off, slap us on the back, and be all "hail fellow well met"! Not until he gets used to us. It doesn't mean he's unfriendly. But her! . . . Did you see those eyes!

IVANOV

Yes. She had two of them.

KUZOVKIN

Are you trying to make me lose my temper?

IVANOV

Dear lord! It's him again.

KUZOVKIN

So what? (*lowering his voice*) Remember who you are . . . (TREMBINSKY *and* PYOTR *come in.* PYOTR *carries a tray.*)

TREMBINSKY

And don't drop anything. Give me that . . . I'll do it. (*takes tray*) Go and get the wine. The wine! (*exit* PYOTR. TREMBINSKY *talks, half to himself, half to* KUZOVKIN *and* IVANOV.) If you want

anything done right, do it yourself—that's what I always say. I
never stop. It's all right for some people—everything handed
to them on a plate—take, take, take—

KUZOVKIN

Are you addressing me, Nartzis Konstantinitch?

TREMBINSKY

I'm not sure I was addressing anybody, sir. Just humbly getting on with my job as usual—(*enter* PYOTR *with champagne
bottles in a huge ice bowl. He places them on a side table.*) And
what the hell are you playing at? Where's the white wine?

PYOTR

I've brought the champagne.

TREMBINSKY

Well, get the wine—the white wine! What d'y think they're
gonna drink with their fish? Don't you know nothing? And before you do, get rid of that draughts board, cluttering the place
up. It's not the time for fun and games . . . (*goes into the hall*)

IVANOV

(*softly*)
That does it. I'm off.

KUZOVKIN

No, please stay. I need you here.

PRASKOVYA IVANOVA

Nartzis Konstantinitch—

TREMBINSKY

What now?

PRASKOVYA IVANOVA

Where's the master?

TREMBINSKY

How should I know? Pyotr, where's he gone?

PYOTR

He's having a look round with Monsieur Tropatchov—

TREMBINSKY

What?

PYOTR

The threshing floor, the sawmill—

TREMBINSKY

Not the sawmill!

PYOTR

What's up? You bin selling off the logs again? (*Clearly he has.*) I'll get the white wine. (*exit; enter from the garden* YELETSKY, TROPATCHOV, KARPATCHOV)

TREMBINSKY

Holy Saint Basil, pray for me—

YELETSKY

And so—

TROPATCHOV

Now what's for lunch? Aha! What have we here? (*lifting covers off dishes*) Kouliabaki—good—sturgeon—good! Comme c'est bien servi! Truly, a banquet! Woodcock—hmmm. One could not hope to dine better at St. Georges. What a crook that St. George is, by the way. I have spent fortunes in his restaurant— Still he is the best. Et noblesse oblige—to always have the best. Shall we sit down? Wouldn't you say so, Kuzovkin?

KUZOVKIN

I'd say it had more to do with breeding than feeding, sir.

TROPATCHOV

Oh would you! (*enter* PYOTR *with wine*)

TREMBINSKY

Give me that.

YELETSKY

Pyotr—

TROPATCHOV

Set the chairs, boys. (TROPATCHOV *and* YELETSKY *sit next to each other at the head of the table.* TREMBINSKY, PYOTR, *and the servants fuss around them.*) Come and join us, Little Fish. That's all right isn't it? Vous permettez?

YELETSKY

Of course. (*To* KUZOVKIN *and* IVANOV) You, too, gentlemen—
to your places. Be seated.

KUZOVKIN

You're too kind . . . but we could not presume . . . We'd be
happy to stand.

YELETSKY

Nonsense! You're my guests. Please, do me the honor—(*He
stands and insists on* KUZOVKIN *and* IVANOV *taking their place
at table. When they are seated, the servants whip the covers
off the silver dishes.*) Now what have we here?

TROPATCHOV

Oh I say! (*his mouth full in no time*) This is superb! Parfait,
parfait!—my compliments to your chef.

YELETSKY

Well, this is a surprise. So . . . We were discussing the estate—
you think I should be making a fortune from the timber?

TROPATCHOV

You could make more from your forests, yes . . . I drink to
your health and happiness, Pavel Nikolaitch—

YELETSKY

Too kind—

TROPATCHOV

Your turn, Little Fish—give him a health.

KARPATCHOV
(*springs to his feet automatically*)

Long life and prosperity to our gracious host . . . (*drains the
glass*) May the heavens rain blessings . . . (*sits*)

YELETSKY

Thank you.

TROPATCHOV

You know what I'm thinking, Little Fish? I'd say we've found
the man we're looking for—the very man. My dear, the nobility in these parts have no spokesman—

KARPATCHOV

Yes indeed. The chair has been vacant too long—

TROPATCHOV

We need a leader of society who can preside at council meet-
ings, speak to government commissions, the privileges com-
mittee, organize the ceremonials, that sort of thing—

YELETSKY

I—a stranger in the district?—no, no, no—

TROPATCHOV

But, my dear, who better?

YELETSKY

My duties at the Ministry would not permit—

TROPATCHOV

Ah yes—the Ministry—this salmon is rather good too—it was
just a thought . . . I think you'd be splendid in the role,
though—raise the tone of the place—show the country clods
how things are done Petersburg fashion—

YELETSKY

Come, come—

TROPATCHOV

No, I mean it—What about you? Don't you agree? Why aren't
you proposing a health to Pavel Nikolaitch—it's your turn?

KUZOVKIN

(*hesitates*)
I hope Pavel Nikolaitch does not doubt the sincerity of my
welcome . . .

TROPATCHOV

Fill his glass, Fishy. Fill it, I said—a brimmer! Now let's hear
what you have to say.

KUZOVKIN

(*stands*)
From a poor man . . . who has nothing of his own to give but kind
words . . . I offer the welcome of a good heart and wish . . . for
our noble host . . . and his dear wife, good health, prosperity, and
measureless happiness . . . (*He bows, drinks very sparingly and
sits.* IVANOV *remains seated but drinks too, and bows.*)

YELETSKY

Thank you, Vassily Semyonitch—very moving—

TROPATCHOV

A little long-winded—but well said! Bravo! (*to* YELETSKY) The trick is to get him drinking—then you'll see some fun— So tell me—er—

KARPATCHOV

Vassily Semyonitch—

TROPATCHOV

Vassily Semyonitch—I've heard nothing of you for ages. How've you been keeping?

KUZOVKIN

I've been keeping well, thank you.

TROPATCHOV

Content with your lot?

KUZOVKIN

I am.

TROPATCHOV

And the famous court case? Is it over yet? A judgment in your favor perhaps? Am I addressing the Lord of Vyetrovo?

KUZOVKIN

(*pause: under his breath*)
Yes—you must find it very funny—

TROPATCHOV

No! Perish the thought! My interest is genuine. The case fascinates me. I tell you I have been at dinner parties where your claim on the Vyetrovo estates has been the sole topic of conversation. What's the latest?

KUZOVKIN

Nothing.

TROPATCHOV

I'm sorry. Sincerely. I didn't know. No progress at all then?

KUZOVKIN

None.

TROPATCHOV

The thing is—never lose faith—have patience—endure. It will come out right in the end. (*to* YELETSKY) My dear, perhaps you did not know, but Monsieur Kuzovkin here is a gentleman of rare breeding—nobler than the whole pack of us no doubt—and heir—the lawful heir, mind you—to the great estates of Vyetrovo.

KUZOVKIN

No, no—it's a very small estate—

TROPATCHOV

How many serfs do you own?

KUZOVKIN

At the last census there were fifty-two.

TROPATCHOV

Really? And how much land?

KUZOVKIN

Well, quite a bit will go in inheritance tax . . . but my claim is for just over two hundred and fifty acres.

TROPATCHOV

And fifty-two serfs to farm them for you?

KUZOVKIN

The lawsuit has been going on for so long—I imagine many of them have gone.

TROPATCHOV

Run away, you mean?

KUZOVKIN

I'm afraid so.

YELETSKY

So why don't you just go and take possession?

KUZOVKIN

Because of the lawsuit.

TROPATCHOV

Yes, Pavel Nikolaitch, probably the most fascinating case in legal history. (*pulls a face at* YELETSKY, *indicating he means the opposite*)

YELETSKY

A lawsuit with whom?

KUZOVKIN

There were other claimants.

YELETSKY

And how long has it been before the courts?

KUZOVKIN

Twenty-six, twenty-seven years perhaps. (*pause*) I have never had sufficient money to pay the tax arrears on the land, nor the solicitors' fees, nor securities into court— Nor do I have any expertise in legal affairs. I can never bring matters to a head. I do what I can, but I suspect that in the end the lawyers will have it all.

TROPATCHOV

Little Fish, give the poor man a drink—

KUZOVKIN

(*hand over glass*)
No. Thank you.

TROPATCHOV

I won't be refused. Fill his glass. (*he does*) I drink to your legitimate claim, sir. May your case have a happy ending. (*drinks.* KUZOVKIN *also drinks and bows to him.*) But you can't go on like this. What if you lose? After twenty-seven years! It's unthinkable.

KUZOVKIN

I can do no more. There hasn't been a hearing for over eighteen months now.

TROPATCHOV

Outrageous!

YELETSKY

Who is acting for you?

KUZOVKIN

(*very reluctant to discuss it*)
There is someone. I have placed the whole affair in his hands—my hopes too—but . . .

TROPATCHOV

What's his name? Which firm is he with?

KUZOVKIN

His name is Ivan Ivanovitch Lytchkhov.

TROPATCHOV

Never heard of him.

KUZOVKIN

Well, he's not . . . He is not a qualified attorney . . . He's more an amateur of the law. It's a passion of his—and he knows more about legal precedent than many a high court judge . . . Since he retired he has had more time to devote to my case . . .

YELETSKY

He's retired?

TROPATCHOV

Really? From what post?

KUZOVKIN

He was a signalman, sir.

YELETSKY

Signalman?

KUZOVKIN

Yes. On the railway.

YELETSKY
(an effort not to laugh)
And he's promised to help you all he can?

KUZOVKIN

He's a good man. I was godfather to his second son. What he doesn't know about the law, he says, is not worth knowing . . . But since his . . . Last year he suffered a stroke. Now . . . he does all he can . . . But . . .

TROPATCHOV

Poor man! That must have been a blow to you?

KUZOVKIN

It was. He has a heart of gold. For years he has labored on my behalf—never asked for any reward. It makes me ashamed to think of his selflessness. I have no way of repaying him, you see.

TROPATCHOV

When did you last have a consultation?

KUZOVKIN

I've not been near him for—oh, it must be over a year. I want to, of course. But I know that he's been unable to make much progress. Yes, I want to see him—as a friend—but I fear that he would reproach himself . . . and . . . the embarrassment . . .

TROPATCHOV

Tricky one, that . . . But you can't just let things slide, y'know? (*motions* KARPATCHOV *to fill* KUZOVKIN's *glass*)

KUZOVKIN

There's nothing I can do.

TROPATCHOV

Well the case can't be all that complicated. Perhaps you'd care to outline the points in dispute? I'm sure Pavel Nikolaitch would find it most enlightening. (*winks at* YELETSKY)

KUZOVKIN

It's really very simple. (IVANOV *gives him meaningful signs to shut up.*) But perhaps not.

YELETSKY

Do tell us. I'd be most interested. I may even be able to help.

KUZOVKIN

As you wish. (*He speaks hesitantly, then with more confidence about a case which has absorbed him for twenty-odd-years. The joke is that his audience lose the thread after a couple of lines, and the argument becomes more and more complex.*) Do stop me if there is any point on which you need clarification. I'm not sure how well I can explain—legal matters—

YELETSKY

Just tell us in your own words.

TROPATCHOV

And have another drink first. (KARPATCHOV *fills his glass.*)

KUZOVKIN

No. Forgive me—

TROPATCHOV

Come on. It'll loosen your tongue.

KUZOVKIN

I've no head for it. (*He drinks.* KARPATCHOV *refills the glass.*)
Well, the Vyetrovo estates—the lands in dispute—belonged to
my grandfather, Maxim Semyonitch Kuzovkin, colonel of dra-
goons—he fought against Napoleon at Austerlitz and
Borodino—you may have heard of him?—who left these lands
jointly to his sons, Semyon, my father, and his brother, my
uncle, Niktopolion.

　　(*the pace increases*)

No provision for the division of the estates between the brothers
was made during the lifetime of my grandfather, Maxim Semyonitch—and my father's brother, Niktopolion—remember this
because it has a bearing on the case—died childless . . . Though
Semyon, my father, the elder, predeceased his younger brother,
my uncle, Niktopolion, and their sister Katerina who—(*to*
TROPATCHOV) as you probably know, Monsieur—had married
Porfiry Yagushkin, whose son by his first wife—she was Polish—Ilya—yes, the loathsome Ilya—was the most notorious
libertine in the province, and to whom—no doubt tricked into
it by my Aunt Katerina—she was capable of such things—my
Uncle Niktopolion gave a banker's draft for seventeen hundred
roubles—payable on his death—Nikopolion's, not Ilya's—and
to Porfiry, now his brother-in-law, another draft for the same
amount. Then, from Semyon my father, Katarina obtained, on
the recommendation of Galushkin—who was appointed
assessor of Grandfather Maxim Semyonitch's estates, after he
had deducted his own fee of nearly five hundred roubles—
which, incidentally, he set against a debt to his own wife—a
written promise of a further two thousand roubles to be made
over to Katerina herself, as her share of the estate, if anything
should happen to him. Not that she was legally entitled to anything at all . . . having had no mention in Maxim Semyonitch's
will . . .

　　All may have been well, had Semyon, my father—God rest
his soul—not passed away. So Katerina, Porfiry, Ilya, and
Galushkin went to Niktopolion and asked for payment.

　　What could my uncle do? He explained that no provision
had been made for the division of the estate, which was now

owned jointly by himself and his nephew Vassily—that is . . .
er . . . myself. At this point death duties were demanded by
the state. Yet I could not legally pay my share of the death duties as I was still a minor, and my uncle and his executors
could not pay as he had an interest in the case, and claims of
his own to settle with Katerina, Porfiry and . . . er . . .

TROPATCHOV

The loathsome Ilya?

KUZOVKIN
(*drinks; glass is refilled*)
Exactly. Now he, Ilya that is, formed an alliance with Galushkin
the assessor and took matters into court, where the waters
were muddied by Ilya, who decided to accuse my aunt, Katerina, his stepmother, of poisoning his servant, Akulina. You may
imagine that things were beginning to get out of hand. Nikopolion's whole life was taken up by the case. Writs were flying,
here, there and everywhere, serfs were absconding from the
estate, we were up to our elbows in affidavits . . . The legal
documents filled three rooms, and every sheet of paper cost
ten times its weight in gold . . . The dispute went from the district court to the provincial court, then bounced back to the
district court . . . and then . . . quite suddenly—a resolution!
Everything seemed to fall into place. The clouds began to lift,
the sun came out, and the family smiled again. We were on
the point of settlement. Tensions just evaporated . . . Then
poor Uncle Niktopolion . . . just gave up and died. Nothing
left to live for, I suppose.

What could I do? I asked the court to put me in possession
of my property at Vyetrovo. The court ordered a sale of the
property in order to pay off the tax arrears—an order which was
blocked by the Court of Chancery—but this same court still refused me possession—can you imagine? The Court of Chancery
forbidding the inheritance of a rightful heir? Katerina's slander
case against Ilya had by this time got as far as parliament, and
a German called Hanginmester had bought up the debts and
presented his claims in the district and provincial courts . . .
After this things began to get complicated—
(KUZOVKIN *is stopped short by a shout of laughter.*
TROPATCHOV *shakes with it. The servants join in.*
KARPATCHOV *shows some pity.* IVANOV *sits in silent
anguish.* YELETSKY *smiles.* KUZOVKIN *is confused.*)

YELETSKY

Forgive me, Vassily Semyonitch—and please . . . please continue.

TROPATCHOV

What did I tell you? Isn't it gripping! Go on, go on!

KUZOVKIN

I . . . I'm sorry. I see I'm wasting your time with . . . I'm making myself ridiculous.

TROPATCHOV

Nonsense! I'm sure we're just getting to the really exciting part.

KUZOVKIN

Pavel Nikolaitch doesn't want to be bothered with this trivia—

YELETSKY

I assure you, sir—

KUZOVKIN

No. My problems are of no consequence, gentlemen. I shouldn't be troubling you with my affairs—

TROPATCHOV

You can't leave us in suspense! Boy—Pyotr—give the gentleman another glass of wine. (*to* YELETSKY) Vous permettez?

YELETSKY

By all means—

TROPATCHOV

Didn't I see some champagne there?

TREMBINSKY

Yes, sir—

YELETSKY

Good idea—open the champagne— (KUZOVKIN *feels he is getting into deep water and looks nervous.*)

TROPATCHOV

We are all gentlemen here. Your misfortune is our misfortune—you must not be afraid—a problem shared is a problem halved—so share—I say this champagne is iced to perfection!—vintage too! Mais c'est magnifique! I drink to you, sir! Pavel Nikolaitch—persuade him to go on—

YELETSKY

I too drink your health, Vassily Semyonitch—soon to be lord of Vyetrovo! Come, drink with me, there's a good chap. (KUZOVKIN *drinks*)

TROPATCHOV

That's the style! (*Led by* TROPATCHOV, *they leave the table and continue drinking champagne.* KUZOVKIN *stands, suddenly quite drunk.*) Splendid lunch, Yeletsky. So where had we got to? Who was this German you mentioned—Hanginmester? I don't think we've come across him before.

YELETSKY

I think he's going to be the villain of the piece.

TROPATCHOV

Of course he is—he's a German, isn't he?

KUZOVKIN

He was certainly one of the villains. He bought up the claims from my aunt, Katerina, for a fraction of their face value— some people say he just bullied them out of her—he was just that type—

TROPATCHOV

That's a German for you.

YELETSKY

So what is your aunt doing about it? And her son—Ilya?

KUZOVKIN

Oh they're both dead—long dead . . . That Ilya was a nasty piece of work. He was burnt to death—knocked unconscious in an alehouse brawl by some louts he was gambling with . . . who then burnt the whole place down. Ilya was drunk under a table. He'd just spent a small fortune on a new suit, I re-member . . . that was burnt too . . . (*to* IVANOV) What do you keep pulling my sleeve for? Are you trying to tell me some-thing? It's all right . . . We're among friends.

YELETSKY

Please don't look so worried, Ivanov.

KUZOVKIN

See? (*To* YELETSKY *and* TROPATCHOV) Am I asking too much

gentlemen? Has a poor man no right to justice? Is justice bought and sold? For myself I ask very little—nothing in fact. Nothing is what I've lived on all my life. I just want somebody to tell me if I'm in the right or in the wrong—the estate must belong to somebody . . . I'm the only member of my family left alive . . . except—

IVANOV

Vassily—

KUZOVKIN

Except . . .

TROPATCHOV

Fill his glass—

KUZOVKIN

Oh no. I mustn't have any more—

TROPATCHOV

My heart bleeds to see a gentleman, a fellow, a dear friend in such distress. If there's anything I can do— (*embraces* KUZOVKIN)

KUZOVKIN

You're too kind—I—(TROPATCHOV *embraces him again*) never knew I had so many good friends. I always thought . . . I was . . . dunno . . . a joke.

TROPATCHOV

My dear! The very idea! Little Fish, we must do all we can to assist this poor unfortunate. Embrace him. (KARPATCHOV *embraces him, spinning round with him as if dancing.*)

KARPATCHOV

Vassily Semyonitch, yours to command, sir—yours to command—

KUZOVKIN
(*trying to keep his balance*)
Really sir, this is too much—too kind. Please! Put me down.

TROPATCHOV

A sad story, sir—and a sad story needs a sad song. Do you know—I suddenly feel the need to shed tears—A song to make us cry, sir. A ballade—

KUZOVKIN

Who me?

TROPATCHOV

You, sir.

KUZOVKIN

I can't sing, sir.

TROPATCHOV

That's not what I hear. Little Fish?

KARPATCHOV

You used to sing in the old master's days. (*a chill descends*)

KUZOVKIN
        (*hurt*)
Yes, but . . . It was a many years ago.

TROPATCHOV

Your old master used to make you sing for your supper, didn't he?

KUZOVKIN

Yes. He did . . . I no longer have a voice.

IVANOV

Really, gentlemen—

KARPATCHOV

They used to make you sing before they would feed you. Don't you remember?

KUZOVKIN

I remember.

KARPATCHOV

And dance too.

TROPATCHOV

Dance too! Really? I never knew that. He should be in the circus! I'd say it was extremely ungrateful of you not to sing for us. After all, you've had your feed.

KUZOVKIN

You must forgive me.

TROPATCHOV

I don't know what Pavel Nikolaitch will think of you.

YELETSKY

No, leave him, Flegont Alexandrovitch—

TROPATCHOV

I'd say it was downright disobliging of you—

KUZOVKIN

Please don't think me ungrateful, Pavel Nikolaitch. My voice has gone.

TREMBINSKY

On the contrary, sir. (*they look at him*) I've been told that at the wedding of this gentleman's brother (*indicated* IVANOV) you were the life and soul of the party. They had a job to stop you singing.

KUZOVKIN

But not recently—

TREMBINSKY

Come, sir. It was less than a month ago.

TROPATCHOV

I knew it!

TREMBINSKY

He was doing Cossack dancing too—

TROPATCHOV

What! Then he can't say no. Why do you refuse to sing for Pavel Nikolaitch when you were quite happy to sing at some bumpkin's marriage feast?

KUZOVKIN

Nobody was trying to force me—

TROPATCHOV

Ridiculous! Nobody's trying to force you now. One gentleman requests another for a song—It's pure ingratitude!

KUZOVKIN

Pavel Nikolaitch knows that I'm not ungrateful—no man could be less so. I'm ready to lay down my life—

TROPATCHOV

We don't want your life, man! Just a song—so come on! We're all waiting. (YELETSKY *looks as if he is going to intervene,*

TROPATCHOV *stops him. There is a long pause. Everybody looks at* KUZOVKIN.)

KUZOVKIN
(*sings*)
Sah ein Knab ein Roslein stehn,
Roslein auf der Heiden,
War so jung und morgenschon,
Lief er schnell, es nah zu sehn—

I'm sorry, I really can't go on—

TROPATCHOV
Come on! You were doing fine. Why did you stop?

KUZOVKIN
Forgive me. I can't sing—I absolutely refuse—

TROPATCHOV
You refuse!

KUZOVKIN
I've done my best—I just can't—

TROPATCHOV
I shall have to encourage you. See this glass of champagne? Why don't I pour it down your neck?

KUZOVKIN
No sir! I don't deserve to be treated like this. I'm not a child— and you're no gentleman.

YELETSKY
That's enough, sir. He's upset. You're going too far—

TROPATCHOV
I'm not a gentleman, eh? Sing!

KUZOVKIN
No, sir!

TROPATCHOV
I shall count to three. One!

KUZOVKIN
Pavel Nikolaitch, stop him!

TROPATCHOV
Two!

KUZOVKIN

Why are you behaving like this? What have I done? You call yourself my friend—then you treat me with contempt. I'm a gentleman, sir, not your fool—

TROPATCHOV

Oho! I thought that's exactly what you were.

KUZOVKIN

Leave me alone!

YELETSKY

Come on, this is getting out of hand.

TROPATCHOV

He calls himself a gentleman, but the whole province knows he was nothing more than your father-in-law's pet monkey. And since his master died, he's been doing nothing for his nuts. It's time he started earning his keep again.

KUZOVKIN

You are humiliating me, sir! Pavel Nikolaitch—don't make me sing . . .

YELETSKY

For heaven's sake! Let it drop, man! I don't care what you do!

KUZOVKIN

Oh, don't be angry with me—

YELETSKY

(angry)

I'm not angry with you. Don't cringe like that.

KUZOVKIN

(regaining his dignity; with some force)

I do not cringe, sir . . . If I have behaved disrespectfully, then I ask you, as you are gentlemen, to pardon me. I confess I have been unable to oblige you . . . in the matter of singing . . . Perhaps there will be an occasion when I can make amends . . .

TROPATCHOV

Oh well . . . (pause) A handsome apology. I too behaved badly. Come, sir. Lets drink down all unkindness. (hands him a glass of champagne. He whispers something to KARPATCHOV, who laughs and exits, taking PYOTR with him.)

KUZOVKIN

(relieved)

With pleasure, sir. (IVANOV *tries to stop him, but he downs the
glass of champagne.*) I shouldn't have drunk that. I told you I
have no head for it, and I've . . . And the head I've got's beginning to spin. Ha!

TROPATCHOV

Oh but today's a special occasion. Champagne's an absolute
necessity.

KUZOVKIN

I'd better sit down. *(sits)* I don't want you to think I'm a spoilsport, Pavel Nikolaitch, but neither do I want you to think of
me as a fool. This is your first day here . . . Country life . . .
Your first impressions of us are so important. I'm no longer a
young man. I hurt more easily. I like to be amusing, but I must
be allowed to keep my dignity. That's not too much to ask, is
it? *(He is almost falling asleep.)*

TROPATCHOV

Don't worry, my friend. Soon you'll be master of your own
estate. Then you'll have all the respect you can manage.
(stands. KARPATCHOV *and* PYOTR *come in with a huge paper
dunce's cap. During the next speech* TROPATCHOV *manages to
place it on* KUZOVKIN's *head. Everybody except* IVANOV *and*
PYOTR *is choking back laughter.)*

KUZOVKIN

(eyes closed and nodding)

Oh, it's just a dream. I wish I still believed it. I wish . . . I wish
. . . But the German will have it . . . Hanginmester. Han—
Gin—Mester. He's the one—the winner—winner takes all.
Let him have it if it means so much to him. I have everything
I need . . . I have her . . . I forgive him. God forgive him. God
bless him. . . . God bless. . . . God bless . . . .

IVANOV

(can't bear it any longer. He goes and shakes
KUZOVKIN *awake.)*

Wake up! Wake up! Look what they've done to you!

KUZOVKIN

*(Reaches up and feels the cap; then he covers his
eyes with his hands and sobs.)*

Why? Why! Why do you torture me? What harm have I done anyone?

IVANOV

Gentlemen? I don't think so.

YELETSKY

Oh come on! They meant no harm—can't he take a joke? It's such a little thing to cry over—

KUZOVKIN

A little thing? Is it a little thing, Pavel Nikolaitch? (*He stands up and throws the cap onto the floor.*) The day you arrive—the first day! (*his voice breaks*) This is how you treat a poor man you called your guest. Fortune has broken me, Pavel Nikolaitch . . . Is it necessary that you should trample upon my head? Shame on you, sir! If you knew how much joy I felt when I saw your love for Olga Petrovna . . . and hers for you . . . Why have you destroyed me, sir? Was it kindly done?

TROPATCHOV

Oh stop whining—

KUZOVKIN

And you, sir—shut your mouth, sir!—you infamous, fatuous fop!—nobody's addressing you, so have the goodness to take yourself off! You think you've made a fool of me, but at what cost to your own character, sir? We all see what you are . . . It's to you I'm speaking, Pavel Nikolaitch— I who was your father-in-law's fool. He thought that for a place at his table and a cast-off suit or two he had the right to treat me like an animal—it was more shame to him than it was to me—swine that he was—And are you swine like him, sir? Are you like that? The manners of the Court?—Is this how men behave in St. Petersburg? Well, shame on the lot of you!

YELETSKY

I think you're forgetting yourself, Kuzovkin. You'd better go and sleep it off before you say something you'll regret.

IVANOV

Come on—

KUZOVKIN

Oh, I'll sleep it off all right! Drunk am I? Play fair, Pavel Niko-laitch, who made me drunk? Oh forget it, forget me . . . You've

had your fun—first day you arrive and I'm back in my place—
a laughing stock—face in the custard . . . But there's something I could tell you all that would wipe the smiles from your
faces . . .

IVANOV

Come along, Vassily Semyonitch. That's enough . . .

KUZOVKIN

I know what I'm doing. Why shouldn't he know?

IVANOV

I'll take you to your room—

YELETSKY

Do. He doesn't know what he's saying.

KUZOVKIN

Is that what you think? I may be drunk, but I'm perfectly
capable—p'fctly—of saying what I'm knowing . . . High and
mighty Saint Petersburg Court gentleman. I'm fortune's
fool!—court jester—a beggar . . . But tell me about your lady,
Pavel Nikolaitch? Tell us about the lady you married?

YELETSKY

Get him out of here. He's becoming offensive.

TROPATCHOV

I'm sorry. It's my fault.

(OLGA *appears, unseen by the party, in the inner hall.*)

YELETSKY
(*to* TREMBINSKY)

Get him to his room. (*to* TROPATCHOV) Let's go into the garden.

KUZOVKIN

You've not answered my question. Who is your wife, sir?

YELETSKY

That's enough! Now take him away.

TREMBINSKY
(*takes him by the arm*)

Come along, sir.

KUZOVKIN

Take your serf hands off me, or you'll get the flogging you deserve! (TREMBINSKY *jumps out of the way and cringes.*) You've married Olga Petrovna, haven't you? Child of an ancient and noble family. Hmm? Oh she is, she is indeed. She's my daughter! Mine! (OLGA *disappears*)

YELETSKY

You . . . (*thunderstruck*) You're out of your mind.

KUZOVKIN

Yes, I'm out of my mind . . . Driven out of it! (*runs off, followed by* IVANOV)

YELETSKY

This is madness!

TROPATCHOV

I'm afraid it's how things are . . . in the country.

Act Two

(OLGA's *drawing room. Glass doors out into the garden. It is richly furnished. Flowers. Window seat—the window looks out onto fields. A sofa. An icon on the wall with candles burning. One door opens onto the ground floor of the house; the other leads to* OLGA's *study.* OLGA *is looking through photograph albums, deep in thought.*)

PRASKOVYA
(*She has just asked a question, but received no reply.*)
It's up to you, of course. (*pause*) I've given my opinion. But the choice must be your own. (*pause*) Madame?

OLGA
I'm sorry. I was miles away—what are you saying?

PRASKOVYA
You were deciding which of the girls is to be promoted to lady's maid.

OLGA
Oh . . . Can't you decide for me, Nanny?

PRASKOVYA
Wouldn't be right, Madame. You must choose between the two I've suggested. There's Irina—

OLGA
Which one is she?

PRASKOVYA
The one with the squint. She's a good girl. Been with the family thirty years or more. Or there's Marfa. She's willing. . . . hard-working . . . If you could get her to wash herself regular.

OLGA

What about the pretty one . . . who laughs all the time? Blue eyes, blue dress . . . sky blue?

PRASKOVYA

Sky-blue dress? (*thinks*) You don't mean Sonya, do you?

OLGA

I don't know . . . Do I?

PRASKOVYA

'Course, it's up to you, Madame. You must please yourself—if it's really her you're set on . . .

OLGA

I—

PRASKOVYA

She's a bit of a handful, though. I wouldn't be doing my duty if I kept that back from you, would I?

OLGA

Well, if you think she's unsuitable—

PRASKOVYA

I can't say much for her morals either. Not that I'm one to spread gossip.

OLGA

There was something sunny in her face . . . But if she can't behave herself—

PRASKOVYA

She doesn't deserve the honor. What would the others think? It wouldn't be fair on them, would it? Not that it's any of my business.

OLGA

(*sighs*)
Oh well . . .

PRASKOVYA

Oh, Madame! I can't tell you what a joy it is to have you home! Pretty as a princess—who would have thought it! And such joy you've brought with you. Such joy in this house again! And so like your sainted mother, God keep her dear departed soul in bliss! I kiss the ground you walk on, Madame—

OLGA

That's enough now, Nanny. You mustn't say such things. I'm just the same, you know—nothing's changed. Off you go now—

PRASKOVYA

Is there nothing I can get you?

OLGA

Not at the moment. No thank you.

PRASKOVYA

So you'll leave it to me then to choose between Irina and Marfa—

OLGA

Yes. But . . . No—I need more time to think. Ask my husband to come in here.

PRASKOVYA

Yes, Madame. (*exit*)

OLGA

My husband . . . my husband . . . (*walks about*) My mind won't let it go . . . (YELETSKY *enters, worried for her.*)

YELETSKY

Olya? What is it? (*She does not know how to answer.*) They said you wanted me.

OLGA

I do . . . Paul . . . The walks, down near the lake; they're all overgrown with weeds. All the paths near the house have been cleared—

YELETSKY

Olya—

OLGA

But down by the lake everything's running wild—

YELETSKY

I've already spoken to the gardeners about it—

OLGA

Oh . . . Have you? And I want them to buy some cow-bells—

YELETSKY
Cow-bells?

OLGA
I love the sound of cow-bells. When I was a child—

YELETSKY
Cow-bells? Olya— Something's troubling you . . . If you can't
tell me what it is . . . I . . . (*He goes to the door.*)

OLGA
Oh, Paul!

YELETSKY
I'll come back when you decide what it is you wish to discuss.

OLGA
Oh don't leave me— What are you doing?

YELETSKY
I'm looking through the accounts with Nartzis Konstantinitch.

OLGA
You sound so cold, Paul. Don't be cross with me . . . Poor
Muddler! Is everything in a dreadful mess?

YELETSKY
Dreadful! Worse than I could have possibly imagined. (*They
both smile.*)

OLGA
I'd better let you go then. Perhaps if . . . Shall we go for a
drive in the carriage? Before dinner?

YELETSKY
(*He goes and holds her for a moment.*)
I'd like nothing better. (*He gets as far as the door.*)

OLGA
Don't go, Paul.

YELETSKY
As you wish. (*He stands near the door.*)

OLGA
I feel as if something's come between us—as if you're hiding
something from me—

YELETSKY

I'm not. If—

OLGA

Yesterday. At lunch. There was a . . . a scene. I have to know,
Paul—

YELETSKY

Oh, That's what it is. Yes. (*sigh*) Such a wretched thing to happen on the day we arrive. Everything was perfect until . . . And
I'm afraid I have a conscience about it—I feel it was entirely
my fault—

OLGA

No!

YELETSKY

Yes it was. That clown Tropatchov took it into his head to
make the poor man drunk—heaven knows why—And I could
have—should have stopped it . . . But . . . It was quite amusing at first—nothing malicious—They got him to tell this story
—some convoluted nonsense about his family cheating him out
of his fortune—it really was . . . Funny. (sighs) But then it got
out of hand. We opened the champagne and . . . Well, you can
imagine the rest. I don't know why I didn't kick the lot of them
out—What possessed me to invite Tropatchov to lunch? Oh
my poor Olya! Is this what's been worrying you?

OLGA

What was it— What did Kuzovkin say?

YELETSKY

He was drunk. Who knows what he was saying? I don't think
he knows himself. (*pause*) However . . . I've dealt with the
matter, and now we must put it out of our minds—

OLGA

How have you dealt with it?

YELETSKY

Well, in the circumstances . . . In any other circumstances . . .
We could have pretended not to have heard. There are some
things, you understand, that a gentleman does not choose to
notice. Unfortunately, there were servants present . . . Oh why
should this be so difficult! It's finished with. I've dealt with it.

OLGA

But how?

YELETSKY

I've spoken to Kuzovkin.

OLGA

Poor man. What have you said? I hope you weren't too severe with him?

YELETSKY

I told him that after such a "scene"—isn't that what you called it?—it would be difficult for him to remain under our roof—

OLGA

But Paul—

YELETSKY

And he agrees with me—is in absolute agreement—

OLGA

But you said yourself—you were to blame—

YELETSKY

His remaining here would be as embarrassing for him as it would be for you—for us— So that's an end of it. I'm not a cruel man, Olya—you know that—I'll find a place for him— Everything will be provided—food, money, everything he needs. But I won't have him in my house.

OLGA

Our house, Paul.

YELETSKY

Oh, my darling, I'm so sorry. I know how much he means to you. I like Kuzovkin too. But it's what he wants . . . If only Tropatchov hadn't turned up . . . If only . . . But what's done is done. I've dealt with it. It's finished.

OLGA

It seems as if we're turning him out of his home in order to keep the good opinion of our own servants, and that of a man like Tropatchov. Paul, that seems like punishment to me—a very severe punishment—

YELETSKY

Olya—

OLGA

And I don't wish to punish anybody—least of all Vassily Petro-vitch!— He has lived here for years. He's part of my child-hood, my happiness. I love him—

YELETSKY

I know, Olya. but there are other reasons.

OLGA

Oh? What reasons?

YELETSKY

Reasons I don't choose to discuss. It was only foolishness—yes. But some foolishness has bitter consequences. Please, Olga. Trust me to do what is best for us. I've pondered this very care-fully. And I promise you—it's at his own suggestion . . .

OLGA

I want him to stay.

YELETSKY

It's impossible. Olya, we mustn't let this come between us.

OLGA

Then there's nothing more I can say?

YELETSKY

Believe me, it's for the best. He wants to go. He packed all his belongings . . . Even before I spoke to him about . . .

OLGA

He'll want to say good-bye to me.

YELETSKY

No. You don't want to see him.

OLGA

I shall certainly see him. I have to see him.

YELETSKY

Then it will be against my better judgment—because I know it will cause you pain. He's pathetic. You're sure to feel pity for him—I did—when I saw his few possessions . . . See him then

But you mustn't ask me to change my mind. This has been
more difficult for me than I would willingly admit . . .

OLGA

If you really think he should go, I won't ask you to change your
mind. Ask them to send him to me.

YELETSKY

He may have gone already. (*pause*) Tu es jolie comme un ange
aujourd'hui. (*This is clumsy and mistimed.*)

OLGA

Please hurry, Paul. (*He rings the bell.* PYOTR *comes in.*)

PYOTR

Yes, sir?

YELETSKY

Send Kuzovkin to us, Pyotr. Your mistress wishes to say good-
bye to him.

PYOTR

Yes, sir. (*exit*)

OLGA

Paul, you must not think me rude . . .

YELETSKY

In what?

OLGA

When he comes, I want you to go.

YELETSKY

(*cold smile*)
No, Olya. That would be unwise. I won't hear of it.

OLGA

I don't want you with us.

YELETSKY

That's hurtful, Olya.

OLGA

You know I don't mean it to be. There are things I must say
to him . . . I need to face him on my own.

YELETSKY

(*stares at her*)
Yesterday . . . Did you . . . did you hear . . . anything?

OLGA

(*innocently*)
What? (*She sits in the window and looks out.*)

YELETSKY

Oh, as you wish, as you wish! You know perfectly well I can
deny you nothing. (*Enter* KUZOVKIN, *pale and drawn. He re-
acts to the fact that she is sitting in the window and covers his
reaction with difficulty.*)

OLGA

Good morning. (KUZOVKIN *bows*) Paul?

YELETSKY

All right, all right. (*to* KUZOVKIN) Have you . . . er . . .

KUZAOVKIN

Everything is arranged. Ivanov is here to collect me—I shall
stay with him for a few days and then . . . I'm ready to leave.

YELETSKY

My wife wishes to say good-bye to you . . . Look, Kuzovkin,
I'm sorry for what happened. Now you mustn't keep him,
Olga. I expect he wants to be on his way. Do you hear me?

OLGA

What? I don't know. I expect we shan't be long.

YELETSKY

Well then . . . Goodbye. (KUZOVKIN *bows,* YELETSKY *exits*)

OLGA

Sit down, Vassily Petrovitch. (KUZOVKIN *bows, but will not sit.*)
No, please. I insist. (*He sits. She does not know how to open
the conversation.*) Paul tells me you're going to leave us.

KUZAOVKIN

(*almost inaudible*)
Yes.

OLGA

He says that you think it best— But don't you know how very
unhappy that will make me?

KUZAOVKIN

I would not make you unhappy . . . but I feel . . .

OLGA

Of course, I'll make sure you have everything you need—if it's
really what you want.

KUZOVKIN
(*gets to his feet*)

I'm very grateful—it's far more than I deserve. Oh I . . . (*chokes
back a tear; manages to hide it from her by being hard on himself*) I must say good-bye now, dear Olga Petrovna.   Forgive
me. I have forfeited the right to call myself a gentleman.

OLGA

No, sit down. You're being very hard on yourself. And very
mysterious. I won't part with you like this.

KUZOVKIN
(*sinks down again—sotto voce*)

But you don't know—

OLGA

Then you must tell me, tell me what happened when they
made you drunk.

KUZOVKIN

Your knowing *that* is painful enough for me. I'm sorry!—truly
sorry, what more can I do or say?

OLGA

I have to know why you're so . . . chastened.

KUZOVKIN

Don't! Please don't, Olga Petrovna. Don't ask me to repeat—
I behaved like a fool—I *am* a fool—it's was nobody's fault but
my own.

OLGA

But—

KUZOVKIN

Pavel Nikolaitch has been very generous—I should be pun-
ished, not provided for . . . I shall always remember him in my
prayers

OLGA

A glass of champagne or two? A little foolery? I've lived nine years in St. Petersburg, you know—survived greater shocks than anything a disagreeable lunch party could produce. But what can you have done that's so very terrible?

KUZOVKIN

No, Olga, no. Don't make excuses for me.

OLGA

Did you insult my husband? Or Tropatchov?

KUZOVKIN

Yes . . . I'm afraid I did. Forgive me.

OLGA

Do you even remember—clearly—what it was you said?

KUZOVKIN

No— I—

OLGA

It was something you said, wasn't it?—

KUZOVKIN
(horrified to think that she might know)
I can't say—

OLGA

What was it you said?

KUZOVKIN

What does it matter what a drunken fool thinks or says? What words or thoughts of mine could have any meaning, or sense, or dignity in them? You know what I am—how worthless I am . . . I said—I *always* say—the first stupid thing that comes into this block of a head—

OLGA

But what did you say—what put it in your head?

KUZOVKIN

My own folly put it there! Pure folly! There's nothing more to say. (*stands*) So, you must let me go. Remember me some-times—as we used to be.

OLGA

Is it my husband you're afraid of? I know he can seem cold—
but—oh, if only you knew him as I do . . . Why are you so
afraid to speak to me? Dear Vassily Petrovitch, you've known
me since I was a child—

KUZOVKIN

Don't! Oh! (*He suddenly bursts into tears; at first she does not
notice.*) You mustn't, mustn't . . .

OLGA
(*turns to him and is shocked*)
Oh! Oh, what have I said—

KUZOVKIN

You musn't remind me of those times. Your childhood. I've ruined
everything, haven't I? Ha! (*shakes and gasps for breath. half smiling, half in tears*) For this to happen now—just when you've come
home to me. I'm sorry. I've no right to presume . . .

OLGA

Vassily Petrovitch, what am I to do with you? You haven't ruined
anything. And you could easily put things right again—there's no
need for this . . . this . . . Only you have to tell me . . .

KUZOVKIN

I must go at once. I shall pray for you night and day as I always have. If I could know you are thinking of me sometimes.
. . . (*he bows*) Your most devoted servant.

OLGA

Are you?

KUZOVKIN

Ask me to die for you.

OLGA

No, I won't ask that. (*pause*) I heard what you said.

KUZOVKIN
(*pole-axed*)
What did you hear?

OLGA
(*forcing herself*)
Is it true?

KUZOVKIN

Oh!

OLGA

Tell me the truth?

KUZOVKIN

Let me go.

OLGA

(*holds him*)
It won't do. No. For the love of God—the truth! Don't torture yourself. The truth! Tell me quickly.

KUZOVKIN

You ask . . . (*shakes his head—he can't get the words "too much" out.*)

OLGA

Is it true!

KUZOVKIN

(*almost inaudible*)
Oh yes . . . it's true. (*He sinks to his knees.* OLGA *moves away quickly.* YELETSKY *comes in. He does not see* KUZOVKIN *at first.*)

YELETSKY

Olya? Are you still in here?

OLGA

Please leave us alone, Paul. (*he hesitates*) Paul, I beg you! (*He goes.*) Get up . . . Please.

KUZOVKIN

(KUZOVKIN *rises*)
Olga Petrovna—

OLGA

Sit here—on the sofa.(*pause*) Vassily Petrovitch . . . do you understand what you have said?

KUZOVKIN

I believe I'm going out of my mind. Send me away before I do any more harm. I believe I no longer know what I'm saying.

OLGA

You know very well what you're saying. There's no going back
now. You must tell me everything . . .

KUZOVKIN

How could I begin? . . .

OLGA

Either you have slandered my mother—in which case you will
leave this room this instant and never come near me again . . .
(*He can't bring himself to go.*) You see, you can't do it. You
can't do it. You can't do it!

KUZOVKIN

Merciful God, merciful God! . . .

OLGA

I am in torment! Do you want that?

KUZOVKIN

Not for the world.

OLGA

(*trying to smile*)
We must help each other.

KUZOVKIN

Yes. Yes. I see we must. (*pause*) Only please don't look at me
like that . . . I can't bear it . . .

OLGA

(*soothing*)
Vassily Petrovitch . . . I . . .

KUZOVKIN

(*gently*)
My dear, forgive me, that's not my name. My name is Vassily
Semyonitch . . .

OLGA

(*embarrassed; shrugs nervously; starts to tremble*)
Oh. Vassily Semyonitch . . . You must think me . . . but you
can't expect . . .

KUZOVKIN

No, I don't . . . (*through tears*) I can't speak if you won't help
me.

OLGA

*(She seems afraid of physical contact with him, but
she takes his hand; she is trying to keep control of
her body.)*

You mustn't be afraid. I'm as frightened as you are. More so.
Much, much more. Look at me. I'm shaking. One of us has to
be calm.

KUZOVKIN

It won't be me.

OLGA

I'll be still—very still—and you will begin at the beginning.
Like the stories you used . . .

KUZOVKIN

Oh! *(after a tremendous effort)* I was just twenty. No money.
Rotten education. Your father (OLGA *shudders*)—the man you
call your father—may God be merciful to him—came to my
rescue or I should have been destitute—brought me here, to
this house, said he'd find a government post for me . . . It didn't
happen . . . I just sort of stayed on. I'd been living here for—
oh, about two years—when he met and married your mother.
She was—I believe this with my soul—with my whole being—
an angel. Before you were born . . .(pause) Before you were
born there were two little boys . . . neither of them lived very
long, poor things—how she loved them! . . .

She was, as I said, perfection. She was loved . . . And nobody loved her more than I did. She was my life. I was still
just a boy really—Innocent. Look into your own heart if you
want an image of mine . . . But there is a type of man who
sees in such perfection nothing but a reproach of his own
rottenness. In her presence that man, her husband, began to
feel nothing but a deep loathing of himself. What happened
was inevitable . . .

Other women. Women as dissolute as he was. One in par-
ticular. A devil. He started to spend all his time with her. God
forgive him, while your blessed mother sat, not speaking a
word, hour after hour, night after night, there—in the window,
her book unopened . . . When I came into this room just now
and saw you there, it was her I was seeing—staring at the road
through the fields . . . never moving . . . through the sunset,
watching the moon rise over the wheat.

At last he abandoned her entirely. Went to live in town with his devil and left his angel wife to fend for herself. How she suffered! You see, she could not find the way to make herself stop . . . loving him . . . Imagine it . . . Forgive me.

After six months he came back. His woman had found another lover—thrown him out. Hunting and drinking, that's how he spent all his time. And then . . . he began the long process of humiliation—beatings, yes—but it was more the cruel insults that, at last, started to break her spirit . . .

She would go into the icon room and stand before the holy images, crossing herself . Smiling sometimes. I think then she began to lose her mind. She could hardly eat. The servants moved about the house like ghosts. Can you imagine the strange, unnatural silence? In the evening she would talk to me—here, in this room—all our conversation was about him . . .

Until one night . . . it was as if her heart—her love for him had broken. She turned to me, and after a long, long silence— I knew . . . I knew . . . what she was going to say, and oh . . . very simply and quietly she said: "Vassily Semyonitch, I know how truly and deeply you love me, and I know at last that he has never loved me, and that he will never feel anything for me but loathing and contempt . . . But I feel for you . . . I need . . ." And she laid her head on my breast . . . We were both lost. Olga Petrovna, I can't tell you any more about it. It's not right that I should.

OLGA

And what happened to him?

KUZOVKIN

The very next day . . . I got up early and went out into the fields. I was still in a dream. I remember the skylarks. Somebody—rode over from the next village. Your father, that man had fallen from his horse. They'd carried his body into a priest's house. I watched your mother go off in the carriage. Dear Lord, we thought she would go mad, she was hardly alive herself—right up until the time you were born. And then, as you know, she never recovered—it was as if she inhabited some other, better world. (*he sinks*)

OLGA

And I . . . I am your daughter. (*pause*) Is there any proof of this?

KUZOVKIN

(*shaken*)

Proof? Olga Petrovna, I have proof of nothing—there is no proof! Had I not made such a fool of myself last night the truth would have gone with me to my grave.

When your father—that man died, I tried to run away—but I could not leave her, I could not break from her. And then I was afraid. The world out there terrifies me. Poverty, unkindness . . . the insolence of life. So, God forgive me, I did nothing. But your mother shut herself away. She locked her mind—shut out the world. And I was never man enough to ever look her in the face. Again there are no proofs, Olga Petrovna, of anything.

But what were you thinking? That I should dare to use . . . Olga Petrovna, I was born a gentleman and I have tried to honor my birth. Had you not insisted—but please never imagine that you will hear of this again.

(OLGA *struggles to her knees.*)

OLGA

What can I be sure of now? My husband, my home? I don't even know who I am.

KUZOVKIN

You believe me . . .

OLGA

Yes. And it's a truth that may destroy us all. What can I be sure of now? My husband, my home? I don't even know who I am.

KUZOVKIN

(*gets up quickly*).

You've nothing to fear. I've told your husband that what I said was nothing but drunken nonsense—I've denied everything. I'll go at once—this will soon be forgotten—I shall pray for you always . . . Oh, I have thrown away my last hope of happiness. (*weeps*)

OLGA

Please don't . . . (YELETSKY *come in unseen by either of them*)

KUZOVKIN

Olga Petrovna, Good-bye. (*holding out his hands*) Good-bye.
Good-bye. (*She runs into her study.*) My God, my God!

YELETSKY

Are you ready?

KUZOVKIN

What? Oh—yes, yes . . .

YELETSKY

What have you found to talk about all this while?

KUZOVKIN

Ha! Oh—the old days . . . You can imagine . . . I begged her
forgiveness of course . . . for being drunk . . .

YELETSKY

And are you forgiven?

KUZOVKIN

I hope so.

YELETSKY

You did not ask her to make me change my mind and let you
stay?

KUZOVKIN

Please, don't insult me.

YELETSKY

I'm sorry . . . I hope you understand, Vassily Semyonitch, that
there is no other way—

KUZOVKIN

Yes, yes. I have not deserved your kindness.

YELETSKY

I am not to blame in this . . . If there is anything you need,
now or in the future, don't hesitate to write to me. I will give
instructions to the people you are going to, but if there is anything. Just write . . . (PYTOR *enters.* KUZOVKIN *bows*) Good-
bye then, Vassily Semyonitch. (KUZOVKIN *starts to go*)

PYOTR

Sir, Flegont Alexandrovitch is here.

YELETSKY

Tell him I am not at home.

PYOTR

Er . . . I'm afraid he's gone into the billiard room, sir.

YELETSKY

Well send him packing!

PYTOR

Yes, sir.

YELETSKY

No, Pyotr, wait . . . You'd better show him in.

PYTOR

Yes, sir. (PYTOR *bows and exits*)

YELETSKY

As Monsieur Tropachov is here, you will oblige me in one more thing. You will repeat to him the denial you made to me this morning. And, as you are a gentleman, you will apologize for the insult you offered him. "Infamous, fatuous fop," is, I believe what you said.

KUZOVKIN

I did. (*To himself.*) How one has to pay for telling the truth! (PYTOR *shows in* TROPATCHOV)

PYOTR

Monsieur Tropatchov, sir.

YELETSKY

Well, did you win?

TROPATCHOV

My dear, I always win. Karpy can't play billiards to save his life, and Ivanov refused me altogether—he says he has a headache—can you believe it, a headache! One would never suspect his head got enough use to make it ache, would one? Now tell me—where is Madame ?

YELETSKY

She'll be here in a moment.

TROPATCHOV

I'm so looking forward to showing you both in society, such as it is . . . Oh? It's you.

KUZOVKIN

(*He bows very formally.*)
Yes—it's me.

YELETSKY

Yes . . . Vassily Semyonitch is a little out of sorts today. He's spent the morning begging everybody's pardon.

TROPATCHOV

Quite right. Well, sir? Have you anything to say to me?

KUZOVKIN

I humbly beg that you will forgive my boorish behavior. I should never have referred to you as an infamous, fatuous fop.

TROPATCHOV

Yes, yes! Well, we'll say no more about it. Even the best families have a little madness in them. You must be allowed to live out your fantasies—I mean, what else is there for you to do? Beyond belief, but harmless enough.

YELETSKY

Well there we are! Friends again.

TROPATCHOV

Now when are you going to let me take you shooting?.

YELETSKY

Well not for some time. There's a great deal to be done on the estates. Things here are not as I would have wished.

TROPATCHOV

Oh but all work and no play you know—so call on me any-time. No ceremony between friends. Let's ask Little Fish; he knows far more about my estates than I do. First-rate shot too. To tell you the truth, I own so much of Russia's dirt that

I can't possibly keep it all in my head. (*at the door*) Karpy! Karpy, come in here!— And we must send to my gunsmith in Petersburg—You must have everything of the best. (*enter* KARPATCHOV) Karpy, I'm going to take Pavel Nikolaitch shooting tomorrow. Where are the best places?

KARPATCHOV

We could walk up the marshes at Koloberdovo. Should be plenty of snipe there by now.

YELETSKY

Tomorrow might not be—

TROPATCHOV

Oh don't be such a spoilsport! Ah! My mouth is watering already. A brace of jack-snipe on a slice of toast, and I'm in paradise.

YELETSKY

Is it far?

KARPATCHOV

Twenty miles by road. Much less cross-country.

YELETSKY

I can't promise— (PRASKOVYA *comes out of* OLGA's *study.*)

TROPATCHOV

Oh come on! We'll make an early start—early as you like, my dear. Up with the lark—the snipe, I should say! Ha, ha, ha!

YELETSKY

Hmm?

PRASKOVYA

(*with a bow*)
The mistress wishes to see you, sir.

YELETSKY

What about?

PRASKOVYA

I couldn't say, sir.

YELETSKY

Very well. (*exit* PRASKOVYA) Gentlemen, you must excuse me.

TROPATCHOV

Of course.

YELETSKY

I won't be a moment. (*To* KUZOVKIN.) I'll say good-bye then.
I expect your friend Ivanov is wanting to be off? (*exit into the study*)

KUZOVKIN

Oh yes, good-bye, Pavel Nikolaitch. (*wanting to escape*) I
must go—

TROPATCHOV

Oh no you don't! You have things to tell us.

KUZOVKIN

I'm afraid you're mistaken.

TROPATCHOV

You're not still feeling embarrassed, are you? My dear, we've
all made fools of ourselves in our time. No wait—wait! Whatever put it into your head that you were her father?

KUZOVKIN

You are perfectly aware what put it into my head. I was drunk.

TROPATCHOV

Queer sort of notion, though?

KUZOVKIN

Drunken fantasy.

TROPATCHOV

More like wishful thinking.

KUZOVKIN

Oh, I do a lot of that.

TROPATCHOV

You've got taste, though. I'll say that for you. Eh, Karpy?
Don't you agree? If a man's going to dream up a daughter, he
might as well dream up one worth dreaming of.

KUZOVKIN

Good-bye, sir.

TROPATCHOV

But why did you lose your temper like that? Let there be no secrets between us. There's more in this—something you're keeping back.

KUZOVKIN

I've said I'm sorry. I really must go.

TROPATCHOV

Oh well. If you won't tell, you won't tell. Though there is a likeness you know . . . I expect that's what gave you the idea? (KUZOVKIN *will not be drawn.*) I say, why don't you come over to my house one evening? Change of feed? You'd be among friends.

KUZOVKIN

Thank you.

TROPATCHOV

It's the place to be. We get up to all sorts, my dear. Ask Karpy—he'll tell you. You'd make a great hit with my guests. You could give us all the latest on the famous court case.

KUZOVKIN

Forgive me. I really must—

TROPATCHOV

Well then, if we must part, we must. Embrace him, Karpy. A fond farewell. Embrace him! You know how! (*He expects* KARPATCHOV *to spin him round again.*)

KARPATCHOV

Good-bye, sir. (*taking his hand;* YELETSKY *comes out of the study and stands unnoticed*) I sincerely regret my part in yesterday's unfortunate affair. I hope you will not think badly of me. (KUZOVKIN *shakes his hand.*)

TROPATCHOV

(*annoyed*)

That's no good, Karpy! I said embrace him. This is how it's done—

YELETSKY

For God's sake, Monsieur Tropatchov! . . . I believe I've told you to leave Vassily Semyonitch alone . . .

TROPATCHOV
(shocked by his tone)
You've told?—

YELETSKY
Yes, sir—told you, sir!

TROPATCHOV
I'm sorry . . .

YELETSKY
I'm surprised that a man of your birth and breeding should
find it necessary to inflict his folly upon so poor an object. I
will not mention this again, sir.

TROPATCHOV
But of course . . . Pavel Nikolaitch! If I have given offense . . .
With all my heart I . . . You must excuse me. I had not real-
ized you were so upset by—

YELETSKY
Leave it, sir.

TROPATCHOV
As you wish. Is it Olga Petrovna? Has something—

YELETSKY
Leave it! No, no. It's nothing. Please ignore my rudeness.
There is a great deal on my mind— *(sighs)*

TROPATCHOV
Of course. We'll leave at once—come, Karpy.

YELETSKY
No, no! You mustn't go! *(trying to smile)* What can you be
thinking of! Please bear with me. I'm not myself this morning.

TROPATCHOV
Don't give it a moment's thought, my dear. Clearly something
disturbing has occurred. I only hope that your dear wife is not
unwell. (KUZOVKIN *is alarmed.*)

YELETSKY
She's perfectly well, thank you.

TROPATCHOV

And I have behaved badly again. It is a weakness of mine to
be overfamiliar with hoi polloi. You are right to admonish me.
(YELETSKY *is like stone.*) It's living too long in the country
that's to blame. The proximity of the pigsty stifles the sensibil-
ities. Eventually people start behaving like animals. All belly
and genitals—

YELETSKY

Please, let's talk about something else.

TROPATCHOV
    (*uncomfortable pause*)
I'm thinking of spending the winter in Paris?

YELETSKY

Are you really? (KUZOVKIN *makes as if to leave.*) No, Vassily
Semyonitch, you may not go yet. There are things I must say
to you.

TROPATCHOV

Paris! Gilded youth! I feel at home there. St. Petersburg can
be so tedious in the winter. Darkness. Silence. Slush. All that
fur . . . I wonder what has happened to Olga Petrovna—

YELETSKY

She will join us in a moment. (*suddenly stands up*) But in the
meantime, perhaps you would prefer to take a turn in the garden?

TROPATCHOV

We'd be delighted to accompany you.

YELETSKY

To speak plainly, there is a matter of business I must discuss
with Vassily Semyonitch—a matter too tedious for polite conversation, so—

KUZOVKIN

Oh?

TROPATCHOV

Oh now I understand, my dear. You had only to say—

YELETSKY

I will join you very shortly—

TROPATCHOV

Please, take as long as you like. Karpy, venez ici. I shall take Karpy into the rose garden and amuse myself with your gardeners. Come along, Leetle Feesh, let's go and study pruning. You must never neglect an opportunity for self-improvement.

(YELETSKY *follows them to the glass doors to the garden and closes them behind them. He has been trying to contain his anger, which now bursts out*)

YELETSKY

And now, sir! Yesterday I regarded you as a drunken fool, today I find you are a liar—don't interrupt me! This morning you told me your story was pure fiction—drunken fantasy— but now I find that you have repeated your lies to my wife!

KUZOVKIN

Pavel Nikolaitch . . .

YELETSKY

Now—finally— Let's have the truth. (KUZOVKIN *is silent.*) Admit it to me—your story is all lies—

KUZOVKIN

Yesterday . . . The champagne—I didn't know what I was saying—

YELETSKY

But today—today you remember perfectly well. How can you look me in the face! Does your sort have no shame?

KUZOVKIN

You misjudge me, sir. Cruelly. What could I possibly hope to gain from—

YELETSKY

I'll tell you what you hope to gain, sir—a fortune! Isn't that what this is all about? By playing on Olga Petrovna's sympathy—either you hope to live on her charity, or it's pure blackmail. (*pause*) Well your plan has succeeded. Yes, I'll meet your terms—buy up the blackmail—on the condition that you take yourself off my estates and never show yourself in the disrict again; (*He leads him to a writing table and sets ink and paper before him.*) that you confess to the lies you have told— Here—sit down, a written confession, and renounce all claim—

KUZOVKIN

I will write no such thing—

YELETSKY

Do you—

KUZOVKIN

And I'll accept nothing from you, Pavel Nikolaitch—Not a kopeck—

YELETSKY

You persist in your lie!

KUZOVKIN

You must think what you like. I will ask nothing, say nothing, write nothing.

YELETSKY

Then what do you want? Surely you can't hope to stay here!

KUZOVKIN

You must let me go—

YELETSKY

Look—take the money. Let Olga believe you lied. Whatever the truth is, let her believe you've made up the story. How can you deny her that peace of mind?

KUZOVKIN

I'll take nothing from you, Pavel Nikolaitch. And I won't lie to her—not to her—not to my—

YELETSKY

My God, man! I'm offering twenty thousand roubles! Surely it's enough!

KUZOVKIN

I won't take it—she knows the truth . . . You'll never see me, or hear from me again. (*tries to leave*)

YELETSKY

Write the confession

KUZOVKIN

Pavel Nikolaitch, let me go.

YELETSKY

I can force you to—

KUZOVKIN

How can you force me?

YELETSKY

Do I have to remind you what you are!

KUZOVKIN

I am a gentleman, sir—

YELETSKY

Some gentleman!

KUZOVKIN

—whose honor, sir, is not for sale.

YELETSKY

Listen to me—

KUZOVKIN

No, sir! I don't choose to listen to you. I'm not one of your St. Petersburg clerks to be bullied and badgered—

YELETSKY

But it's her I'm thinking of! You say you love her— Do you wish to destroy her? Say you lied. I beg you—Accept the money. Even if you can't say the words, it will be enough to convince her of the lie.

KUZOVKIN

No, no, no—She understands—

YELETSKY

Are you so very rich? Does twenty thousand roubles mean so little to you?

KUZOVKIN
(*a moment of real anger quickly suppressed*)
Just accept the fact . . . I'm going away. You will not buy me, sir! I'm not made of saleable stuff !

YELETSKY
(*Deflated—he is finally forced to accept the truth.*)
Dear God . . . Then she is your . . . (TROPATCHOV's *grinning*

face is seen peering through the window. KARPATCHOV *is heard tapping on the glass.*) This is intolerable! (*goes to the window*) I'm coming! I'm coming! Please, a moment longer . . . Think over what I've said—take a few minutes and think of this, Vassily Semyonitch: If you are what you claim you are, tell me, what do you have to offer her? This house will not be her house—this estate—your home for thirty years or more— is neither yours, hers, nor mine. Before you break her heart, sir, think what you would be taking from her—her childhood memories, the honor of her mother, her peace of mind. (*He exits through the door into the garden.*)

KUZOVKIN

Dear God! I'd rather be in my grave. (OLGA *comes out of her study.*)

OLGA

Vassily Semyonitch . . .

KUZOVKIN

(*turns from her*)
Olga Petrovna . . . why did you tell him?

OLGA

I'm his wife now, Vassily Semyonitch. I could never conceal anything from my husband.

KUZOVKIN

Ah . . .

OLGA

I want you here with me. I want us . . .

KUZOVKIN

No, this is no place for me . . . There was a time when this house was all sunlight—a most beautiful garden, peace, birdsong— your voice, dear little Olya. But all that's gone. We can't bring it back again. To your husband, I am a figure of contempt, and to you I'm a stranger. No, don't say anything. A while ago I asked you to think of me sometimes. Now I feel it's best if you forget me completely. I cannot stay. It would drive a wedge between you and your husband.

OLGA

Then . . . take . . . (*Embarrassed, she reveals the letter.*) You must not refuse me. It's . . .

KUZOVKIN

Olya?

OLGA

It's to buy back your estates . . . Vyetrovo . . .

KUZOVKIN

(*drops the letter*)
You too? How can you—

OLGA

Vassily Semyonitch! Listen to me! It's because . . . You are my father! I've known it—here, in my heart—since I overheard . . . Look into my eyes—see! See the truth. (*She embraces him very gently and lays her head on his breast. They stay like that.*)

KUZOVKIN

Oh Olya, Olya . . . (*She kisses him; then she picks up the note and presses it into his hand.*) (*tears*) It's enough that we know—that we both know.

OLGA

Oh my father . . . You cannot refuse your own daughter.

KUZOVKIN

—No, no, I can refuse you nothing. (*He takes the letter.*)

OLGA

(*dries his tears*)
We shall see each other. I shall find a way . . .

KUZOVKIN

It's too much . . . a dream . . . (*He lifts her to her feet.*) Olya. Quickly. Give me your hand . . . for the last time. (*He kisses it; she kisses him; he sinks into a chair; she quickly goes to meet them, wiping her tears; they come in.*)

TROPATCHOV

(*bows*)
Well, well, well! Enfin! A heavenly vision! My dear, how are you today?

OLGA

Thank you.

TROPATCHOV

Actually, to tell the truth and shame the devil, you look quite
drawn. I do hope you're not unwell—

YELETSKY

We're both a little under the weather. The long journey—first
night in a strange house—

TROPATCHOV

Fresh air's what you need— My dear your garden is simply too
lovely. (KUZOVKIN *goes to the window and turns his back on
them.*)

OLGA

It always was.

TROPATCHOV

Perfection—mais c'est très beau, très beau—the pergola, the
rose garden, those exquisite statues—Italian, aren't they?—
Yes, yes! Art and nature—my only vices . . . (*He goes over to
some albums on a table.*)

YELETSKY
(*whispers to* OLGA *inaudibly*)

Has he accepted the money? (*She nods; pained. Joyfully, he
embraces her, and she, repulsed, pulls away, and crosses to*
TROPATCHOV.)

OLGA

What have you found, Monsieur?

TROPATCHOV

A photograph album. Here—yourself as a child—What an
angel! And here you are, as it says at age six. Here you are on
your nanny's lap. Who is that? Is that you, Vassily Semyonitch,
in the background? Is that Madame Kovrinskaya?

OLGA

I don't remember—

TROPATCHOV

You don't remember the Kovrinskys? You must meet them!
My dear, the best table in the district—until you came home,
that is.

YELETSKY

(*to* KUZOVKIN)
You've accepted?

KUZOVKIN

Yes, sir.

YELETSKY

(*To* TROPATCHOV, *who is talking to* OLGA.) Gentlemen, I have news. Only yesterday we were laughing—rather unkindly, I'm afraid—at the complexity of our friend Vassily Semyonitch's court case. Well, today the tables are turned upon us. News has arrived—the good news—the excellent news—that the case is over. The courts have found in favor of Vassily Semyonitch, who may take possession of his Vyetrovo estates as soon as he pleases.

TROPATCHOV

Is this a joke?

YELETSKY

No, I assure you. Ask Olga. See—there are tears in her eyes—tears of happiness.

TROPATCHOV

Vassily Semyonitch, is this really true?

KUZOVKIN

(*smiling like a child*)
Yes, sir.

TROPATCHOV

I'm amazed! What can I say! Many congratulations, my dear! (KARPATCHOV *bows to* KUZOVKIN *and shakes his hand.*) I couldn't be more delighted for you, Vassiy Semyonitch! You must be simply dying to rush off and look the place over, eh?

KUZOVKIN

Naturally.

TROPATCHOV

Ha, ha, ha!

YELETSKY

He's leaving us almost at once.

TROPATCHOV

Oh I'm sure he is! Now that he has an estate of his own, there's nothing to keep him here.

KUZOVKIN

Nothing.

TROPATCHOV

You'll be going into town, then?

KUZOVKIN

Yes. There will be documents to read, papers to sign—

TROPATCHOV

Not a moment to be lost, then! I suppose it's all your lawyer's doing—Mr. Signalman Lytchkhov, wasn't it? The retired gentleman—I suppose he put everything in train! (*Nobody else thinks it's funny.*)

KUZOVKIN

Oh, very good—

TROPATCHOV

You must promise to invite me over for a spot of shooting. What do you say, Karpy?

KUZOVKIN

My friends will always be welcome.

TROPATCHOV

So why aren't we celebrating? Fetch the champagne!

YELETSKY

Yes. Why not. Yes. A little celebration would be appropriate.

PYOTR

(*enters*)

Yes, sir.

YELETSKY

Tell Trembinsky to fetch some champagne.

PYOTR

At once, sir.

YELETSKY

And is Monsieur Ivanov still here?

PYOTR
He's waiting in the linen cupboard, sir.

YELETSKY
In the linen cupboard? Ask him to come in here.

PYOTR
Yes, sir. (*exit*)

TROPATCHOV
Oh my dears! What times we shall have! There's more fun to be had here than at the theatre! Karpy, you can forget Paris—we'll stay home this winter. There'll be such stories to tell. I shall make it my mission to introduce you both to all the best houses in the district. (*going over to* OLGA, *who has all the time been looking at the daguerreotypes and at* KUZOVKIN) We'll start with the Kovrinskys. You will adore Madame Kovrinskaya, my dear, and she will adore you. She was very close to the Tsar, you know. Closer than she cares to admit, but I adore her. We shall all adore each other.

OLGA
(*forced smile*)
Ah!

(TREMBINSKY *comes in followed by* PRASKOVYA *and the other servants with the glasses;* PYOTR *carries the champagne;* IVANOV *follows timidly.* OLGA *greats* IVANOV.)

TROPATCHOV
Ah the champagne! A toast to Vassily Semyonitch!

OLGA
(*to* IVANOV, *who bows to her*)
I'm very glad to see you, Monsieur. You must be very pleased for your friend . . . has he told you? He has come into his estate. (IVANOV *bows again, goes over to* KUZOVKIN; PYOTR *and* TREMBINSKY *pour and hand round the champagne.*)

IVANOV
What nonsense is it this time?

KUZOVKIN
Shhh, Vanya. There's no need. It's all right.

IVANOV

But what's happening—

KUZOVKIN

Nothing. Everything.

TROPATCHOV

Well, there's only one possible toast: A health to the new lord
of Vyetrovo! Joy and good fortune!

ALL *(except* IVANOV)

Joy and good fortune!

KARPATCHOV

I wish you all happiness, sir. (*He looks hard at* TROPATCHOV.
YELETSKY *nods, and the servants begin to slip discreetly from the
room.*)

KUZOVKIN

(*in a dream*)
On this day of days . . . allow me to express my thanks for all
your kindness—

YELETSKY

You've nothing to thank us for, sir—

KUZOVKIN

You are head of this family now—this family has provided for me
for over thirty years—of course I must thank you. As for my behavior yesterday—I ask you all to forgive me . . . and to forget . . .

YELETSKY

It's not necessary. You've said enough . . .

KUZOVKIN

As I shall forget. I take no offense. A gentleman does not
choose to notice the slights, indignities, calumnies, and insults
that are heaped upon him day after day, year after year, by
infamous, fatuous . . . Forgive me. A real gentleman must be
able to suffer a joke at his expense with dignity even when the
whole world is laughing at him. Eh? Is that not so, Tropatchov
—Wouldn't you agree, my dear? So . . . What more is there to
say? Good-bye. That's all.

(KUZOVKIN *bows to them, still smiling;* IVANOV *is suspicious;* YELETSKY *wants to have done with it;* OLGA *on the verge of tears. The servants are dumbfounded.* KUZOVKIN *takes leave of them.* PYOTR *weeps. Finally he stops at* TREMBINSKY. TREMBINSKY *bows deeply.*)

KARPATCHOV
Surely, sir—It's not good-bye. You're not exiled to Siberia, you know . . .

KUZOVKIN
(*moved*)
Of course I'm not . . . All that's left to me is happiness. (*through tears*)

YELETSKY
(*mutters to himself under his breath*)
For God's sake, go!

OLGA
(*goes to* KUZOVKIN)
Good-bye, Vassily Semyonitch.

KUZOVKIN
God be with you, Olya . . . (*kisses her hand*)

YELETSKY
Come, come! Let's have no tears. Come . . . Good-bye.

KUZOVKIN
Good-bye. (*bows; goes slowly to the door—all go out to see him off. Except* OLGA, *who comes downstage.*)

TROPATCHOV
(*off*)
Give our regards to Vyetrovo! (*The men, except* IVANOV *and* KARPATCHOV, *come back; first* YELETSKY, *then* TROPATCHOV, *who slaps him on the back.*) You didn't fool me for a minute! You're giving him his marching orders—But with what delicacy you do it! The truth is . .. you bought it for him, didn't you? That's what I call handsome! How very generous—you're a gentleman, sir.

YELETSKY
It was nothing. You're too kind.

TROPATCHOV

Nothing he says? Well I must say—

YELETSKY

Nothing, Monsieur. Nothing. Let that be an end of it.

(OLGA *watches from the window.* YELETSKY *firmly ushers out* TROPATCHOV, *then goes and pours himself a stiff drink, watching* OLGA. OLGA *comes from the window, ignoring* YELETSKY, *and kneels in front of the icon.*